Internet Empire
The Hidden Digital War

Internet Empire
The Hidden Digital War

Sean F. Ennis

Islington Green Publishing

www.TamingTheGiants.com

Published by Islington Green Publishing
20-22 Wenlock Road, London

Islington Green Publishing

First edition

Book cover design by ebooklaunch.com

ISBN: 978-1-7396922-3-0/paperback
ISBN: 978-1-7396922-4-7/hardback

DEDICATION

Dedicated to my parents, Helen and Robert, and to my wife, Valérie, who have made this book possible.

CONTENTS

ACKNOWLEDGMENTS

Many thanks to colleagues, friends and teachers with whom I have discussed, learned, agreed, and sometimes – if not often – disagreed. For your contributions to the Socratic process you encouraged, I thank you. You know who you are. Particular thanks go to colleagues at the European Commission's DG Competition, the Organisation for Economic Co-operation and Development (OECD), the US Department of Justice Antitrust Division, and the University of East Anglia (UEA). I am also grateful for the feedback from colleagues during presentations at the University of Amsterdam, BECCLE, CRESSE, Cambridge University, DigEcon, the European Association of Research on Industrial Economics, the International Competition Network, London School of Economics, and UEA. Special thanks to Cyprien Denolle and James Zuo for their research support, careful reading and comments. Finally, I deeply appreciate lively discussions with staff from competition authorities, internet companies, and law firms with whom I have worked.

INTERNET EMPIRE

PREFACE

Behind a provocative title stands a challenging set of questions.

This book is not intended as an unremitting condemnation of the companies that have come to dominate the internet economy. These predominantly US-based companies have come out on top through excellent management and superb translation of innovations into new products. They operate in a country that provides a better infrastructure for innovation, corporate finance and financial rewards than other countries. The resultant magnetic power of Silicon Valley attracts digital workers from around the world like Hollywood attracts actors. While at times these powerhouse companies have acted at the expense of consumers, businesses and other governments, they have fundamentally demonstrated the ability to implement new business models and deliver major innovations.

US companies have won many battles in the war to control the value generated by the new digital economy. The analogy I make with war is not incidental. While the US global dominance has been achieved without large-scale physical violence or resistance, many of the traditional goals of war have been sought and won. Understanding the differences and similarities to classical wars is a starting point for understanding what has happened to modern economies.

While these companies have brought together a new order, they are all quite different. The media, governments and courts have criticized them for abusing their power and at times creating societal and personal harms. But the policy problems related to their behaviors are distinct. A one-size-fits-all regulatory approach cannot be appropriate to answer the policy challenges posed by companies operating in various sectors of the economy and which differ greatly in their business models and societal impacts.

While many accusations against these companies are unfounded, many others are on track. This book is not here to separate the wheat from the chaff, nor is this a witch-hunt. Instead, this book intends to explain the key economic impacts of the online world, the key forces behind the success of US tech companies and what we can do to solve the challenges they have created. The negative impacts generated by the internet companies can be only partially addressed by governments. The reason is that our individual usage of these products gives rise to these impacts.

Most of us are avid consumers of the Internet. Under the influence of limited options available to us, we have chosen what services to use and when. We have selected our favorite platforms and apps to help us navigate complex choices and information. The array of choices has sometimes been straightforward, sometimes overwhelming. But ultimately the choices have been our own. Therefore, we are not blameless. Have you ever wondered how your own personal actions fit into this picture? How did we collectively make this takeover possible? How have governments influenced the outcomes? What can we do to improve the situation?

If you would be interested in answers to these questions, then this book is for you.

First, we will immerse ourselves in the backstage operations of this new and civilized type of World War which fortunately is in such stark contrast to real war. Then we will recognize the multifaceted economic impacts from digitalization. Finally, we will embark on a journey to figure out how we can achieve the key benefits of internet services while making them fairer and better.

The questions here are simple. So are the answers. The challenges are too crucial to rely on a distant government. Rather, we must rely on ourselves – on each one of us alone, and on ALL of us together – as we personalize our reactions to the Internet Empire.

If we will not endure a king as a political power, we should not endure a king over the production, transportation, and sale of any of the necessities of life. If we would not submit to an emperor we should not submit to an autocrat of trade, with power to prevent competition and fix the price of any commodity.

-Senator John Sherman (21 Cong. Rec. 2,457 (1890))

War's a game which, were their subjects wise, King's would not play at.

-William Cowper

1. AND SO IT BEGINS…

In the country of the blind the one-eyed man is king.
-Desiderius Erasmus

A war has been fought and won in a subtle and modern style of battle. The hearts and minds of the disputed territory have been taken over. As with all wars, there have been winners and losers. In this case, the losers are many – and, frankly, sometimes deserved to lose. The winners, on the other hand, are shining beacons. The hidden war I am talking about is for control over the commercial internet economy. The winners include household names of the Internet.

The leading companies involved are sometimes called the GAFAM (Google (Alphabet), Apple, Facebook (Meta), Amazon and Microsoft). But in a sense, lumping together these companies is inadequate, as they are very different from each other, and the arguments of this book also apply to many other smaller companies. Nonetheless, for most readers these leading companies have become a mainstay of their daily lives, and other internet companies as well. While governments may portray large internet companies as ignoring the law, these companies are not fundamentally law breakers. They have generally acted within the bounds of the law. In doing so have created amazing new products that engage loyal and enthusiastic followings. Their founders and investors generally deserve their success, but not the benefits of corporate power that keeps out competition. Internet companies are increasingly being sued over alleged violations of laws, such as for restricting competition, paying insufficient heed to privacy or spreading harmful messages. Such allegations are ultimately addressed by administrative bodies and courts, and are therefore not the focus of this book.

We will be focusing instead on what the companies have effectively accomplished, from an international trade perspective, which is truly remarkable. The approach is focused on whether these companies are delivering real value, who benefits from that value and where that value is created.

This immaterial war has profound economic consequences for our futures. In some countries, there has been an enormous loss of control over domestic economic activity. But who has won this war? The unquestionable winner is the United States.

The US and its companies have taken over large parts of the operation of the world's market economies, thanks to the Internet, great management, US government support and a new type of hipster warrior. And while many commentators and politicians have noticed what has happened, and new regulations are fast accumulating to control these companies, few have realized that World War 3.0 can now, officially and finally, be declared over.

The actions lawmakers and courts are taking are too little and perhaps too late. They are too little because they will not fundamentally question the new world order that has been created. They are too late because undoing the extreme market concentration that has been created will not be easy to achieve through legal challenge. It may also be too late to encourage national internet company growth outside the US. These companies have become ingrained in business processes and the way people run their daily lives. That deep envelopment in our lives cannot be changed with a snap of one government's fingers, despite politicians' best wishes.

There are two primary reasons for war: the first is control of economic activity; the second is non-economic and might arise from religious expansion, ideology, ethnic conflicts, creating more defendable borders or pure hubris. The focus of these reflections is on the first rationale: war for economic gain. I argue that the Internet allows for the objectives of war to be realized without a single pitched battle being fought, without soldiers dying, and without a single bomb being dropped. The reason for this is that most of the economic activity and value in modern economies comes from services instead of goods.

Importantly, control over services can be run from a distance. This distant oversight has made possible the most striking takeover of economic activity of one country by another that has ever occurred. The conquering country uses surrogates, corporations whose headquarters it hosts and which it systematically protects. They in turn contribute to the strength of its economy through employment and payment of taxes. These corporations have not been chosen by the government. They have themselves fought it out with actual and potential competitors to rise to the top of their business.

Subtly, without big fanfare, a digital war has been fought, and it has been won. It has been won, hands down, by large US-based Internet companies. It has been won through an assortment of deals sealed with champagne in San Francisco Bay restaurants, in laid-back Seattle coffee houses, in Silicon Valley based law firms and in K Street lobbying firms. This war has been run by computer science PhDs, drinking their double macchiatos late into the night. But above all, it has been fought by pioneers giving people what they want, with tremendous innovation that yields enormous economic power and economic gain for the winners. This war has been won by an army wearing Birkenstocks, not boots, an army that relaxes in the evening with cocktails by their pools. It might seem exaggerated but is not far from the cliché of Silicon Valley startups. This is an amazing war that has been won with the full and enthusiastic cooperation of those who are conquered.

While the gain of this war is not directly into the pockets of the United States government, the nation indirectly benefits through increased tax revenues and employment, as would normally occur in economically motivated wars. US unemployment has decreased, US tax receipts have grown disproportionately, economic activity in the US hubs of activity has grown, projection of US economic power has expanded into a new domain. One aspect of this activity, the largest spying operation in history has been established with hardly a whimper or complaint, as Google and even Pokémon Go have created enormous databases on personal activity and geographic mapping that, were they run by government, would create a furor.

This impressive private sector achievement has been supported by enormous, behind the scenes efforts by the US government to ensure that trade barriers do not develop on the Internet. The focus of such efforts has been in bilateral government lobbying and influencing of multilateral organizations that may have an ability to focus on and address these topics. This has included a major push for a digital trade agreement at the World Trade Organisation (WTO), even while the Trump administration was pulling back from other WTO commitments. More than 75 countries are pursuing this international WTO agreement under the push from the US. The US government also lobbied for the inclusion of e-commerce provisions in templates of the Comprehensive and Progressive Agreement for a Trans-Pacific Partnership (CPTPP) and the United

States-Mexico-Canada Agreement (USMCA). Finally, it conducted bilateral agreements with Japan and other countries. The United States, through its largely free trade dogma that it has espoused over the last 4 decades has created the environment that allowed this difficult to control, almost invisible economic activity to expand.

While the US backtracked on the WTO in almost all spheres under Trump, it maintained the push in that forum for a digital agreement. The reason is simple. The US has a fundamental economic interest to maintain full access to other countries for its world-leading digital enterprises. This rational pursuit of self-interest at a geopolitical level shows that the US is doing its job to represent its own interests. To the extent that a digital agreement is a zero-sum game, it does not admit the possibility for two sides to be winners. The willingness of other countries to enter an agreement is then driven by other factors. These can include a short-term political need for an agreement, an ideological belief that principles in an agreement represent good policy even if their country is a net loser, or domestic pressures from their own digital businesses.

One feature of the WTO understanding on digital trade, which is remarkable, is not allowing countries to stop internet traffic unless its content violates their law. At the Organisation for Economic Co-operation and Development (OECD) and the G20, the US delegations have consistently, and at levels hidden from public view, pushed to avoid significant discussions related to "winner-take-all" internet activities. The United States has pushed for no limits on digital commerce and for a taxation regime that is favorable to US taxation of internet company profits, while also suppressing all significant official international discussion of how to govern, control and regulate the Internet.

The OECD, with strong US government backing, brokered a tax accord between countries in 2016, the Base Erosion Profit Shifting agreement, that embodied the principle that companies should report and pay taxes on their profits in the countries where they are based. The tax agreement effectively suggested that the correct home for taxation of internet businesses with a US headquarters is the US. The Europeans had started negotiating the agreement at a time of much lower digital enterprise profitability than the current level, so the fact that it did not address an adequate sharing of profit taxes would not have seemed an insuperable barrier to the agreement.

The Europeans subsequently pursued ineffective policies to remedy this tax failure. In 2017 the European Commission issued a decision that Apple and Amazon (or Ireland and Luxembourg) had receiving preferential tax deals that allegedly gave the companies an undue competitive advantage. The decision, subsequently in litigation, required that the companies needed to repay the illegal tax benefit to Ireland and Luxembourg.

Seeking broader solutions, France in 2019, Spain in 2021, and other countries, sought to raise transaction taxes on internet sales. While they thought to start taxing internet profits by taxing sales, companies like Amazon turned around and, as a normal company would, comparably raised their charges to companies selling over their marketplaces. With respect to the Spanish tax, in a January 2021 retaliation, the US Trade Representative took action to impose tariffs of 25 percent on selected Spanish goods. The US argued that the Spanish Digital Service Tax restricts US commerce, discriminates against US companies, and violates international tax principles by taxing sales of products instead of income of companies.

While non-US countries may have a desire to tax gains from economic activity happening within their borders, the unilateral tax hikes they impose on US companies are likely an unfair double taxation.

A broader agreement on digital enterprise tax could be a solution but the US government has held back its assent to such an accord. Indeed, the current international tax agreement is highly favorable to its own companies and to itself. The US benefits from the agreement's designation of itself as the producing country of digital services. This designation in turn gives the US the exclusive right to tax its digital company corporate income. Any broader digital tax solution will naturally lead to profits originating from a European country's consumers being taxed increasingly at the source of the consumption, which is in Europe. This would reduce the US government taxation benefits from its corporations' activities overseas.

Even when the OECD brokered an agreement for a minimum corporate tax of 15 percent, that was formally agreed on 8 October 2021 by 136 countries, the Europeans permitted a delay for an agreement on digital taxation. This is an example that illustrates how European countries focus on short-term political gains from policies, while the US (and China) have much better capability to focus on long-term outcomes.

The US government's role in internet policy goes back decades. The Clinton White House pursued a national and international policy push towards an open internet, with key advisor Ira Magaziner saying that the Internet must be left to grow on its own, with no regulation and with government hands kept off its evolution. His initial objective was to prevent the US communications regulator, the Federal Communications Commission, from regulating the Internet, and to prevent telephone companies from controlling it. This US government role in policy could be seen as a continuation of its role in supporting the rollout of the initial technology two decades before, when it financed the development of the first networks of distant computers.

The "Magaziner" principle, has largely permeated policy making worldwide. The principle embodies the view that digital innovation should not be constrained by old-fashioned telecommunications regulation. It had the unforeseen implication that monopoly power obtained through legitimate means would not be subject to regulation.

However, the monopoly power achieved by many of the internet companies is non-trivial and may allow some of these companies to reach into global economic activity in a way that is difficult to challenge. They may compete with each other, but the economic control is often wrested from one US company to another, such as from eBay to Amazon. They are still battling each other, using surrogate companies, in India and other countries where internet markets are growing rapidly.

China, and more recently Russia, has resisted this US takeover of the digital economy. China has placed operating requirements for access to its markets in a way that ultimately allowed its domestic companies to keep a higher degree of independence in the internet area. One impact is that China has a better capacity to maintain control over social communication. This also follows from the Chinese objective to ensure that major economic activities in the country are not taken over by foreign companies.

This book will document the ways in which this international war for the control of economic activity has been won by the United States. It will also point out the irony of this victory: governments can control the internet pipes that operate in their country, as China showed with its active intervention to prevent foreign internet company domination. But most non-US governments have allowed foreign companies (mainly from the US) to gain trade-protected control over their economic activity. They have allowed these companies to meticulously map their geographic space, server locations and internet usage profile of its citizens. They have created an environment in which others are allowed to monitor their own territory, a surefire indication of foreign takeover.

Our voyage will first explore how the commercial internet developed, then examine the remarkable sector-specific impacts on economic activity from the commercial internet, including the at times hidden ways in which internet companies charge for their services and distort information. These will show the nature of the US takeover of internet activity. Next, we will explore the economic rationale in the origins of many wars and prior empire building, ranging from Roman history to the creation of the United States itself. After this, we will explore why the Internet Empire that has been created has many of the same economic consequences as a war, without many of the associated costs, and is therefore more stable in many ways than physical empires. We will then proceed on a path that examines where the Internet is headed, if it continues on the current path. In considering ways for society to respond, we will briefly consider how resistance to empires has been organized previously, and draw lessons on the value of both government and personal action. Possible government responses are outlined as a function of the problems identified, and actual government plans are analyzed for their focus and their weaknesses.

Because of the natural constraints on government action, we finally develop a set of individual actions that can be seen as options for resisting those parts of internet empire building with which you might be uncomfortable. These personal options for taming the Internet accept the tremendous benefits that the Internet has brought to us. But they ensure that for each of us the Internet is harnessed and directed in ways that help to create the future society we want. The options respect both individual and business rights, and ultimately can yield better deals and safer choices for ourselves.

The digital war has created an enormous and decentralized Internet economic empire. Deleterious effects of this war can still be undone. Territory can be brought back under domestic legal and tax control. In many respects, Europe has been asleep at the wheel. Americans have also experienced a takeover of their lives, as most of them are not benefitting as producers from the new economy. The real benefit is to a select few and the US tax base.

The time has come for us, the disaggregated mass of internet users, to wake up and fight to stop any negative elements of this takeover. As in any war that has been won, small tinkering around the edges will not work. Instead, brute force needs to be used, though only focused on the malicious elements. But this force will have many tentacles. Just as this war was not won with bombs, it will not be resisted with rifles. The resistance will involve changed rules by government and changed behavior by users.

Some governments have woken up, with the support of their citizens, to reassert the control over their domestic economic activity. As with any war, resistance can raise the costs to those who have taken over economic activity to such a level that they choose to withdraw or change their style of operation. The challenge is to ensure that, after any successful resistance, the positive features of the Internet remain. These positive features include the enormous efficiency benefits of the Internet and the tremendous innovations in computing remain, grow and even strengthen.

The time to reassert societal control is now. The challenge is to do so in a way that does not hurt us, the internet users, and that does not deprive companies of legitimately earned value. This is why I suggest changing the way *we* behave is the key to a durable resolution. At stake is nothing less than our own future.

2. A SNAPSHOT

No war, or battle's sound,
Was heard the world around
-John Milton

The Internet was born a quiet, unremarkable birth on 21 November 1969 when a connection was created between the SDS Sigma 7 computer at the University of California in Los Angeles and the SDS 940 computer at the Stanford Research Institute. The new creature weighed in at 1800 pounds (or 816 kilos) and measured 311.8 miles (or 501.8 km). Within a month, computers from the University of California at Santa Barbara and the University of Utah were added to create a four-node network. This expanded further over time, as more computers joined.

The private focus of this internet activity is the key to its worldwide success. But what is less well known is that the origin of the Internet itself was, like many new technologies, a product of the US military establishment, and can thus be seen as a creation of the US government. The Transmission Control Protocol (TCP) that underlies internet communications was conceived in 1973 by Robert E. Kahn, who worked at the US Advanced Research Projects Agency (ARPA), and Vint Cerf, who worked at Stanford and later moved to ARPA. Their work built not only on US developments but also French ones, notably the packet communication method built by Louis Pouzin for the French computer network development Project Cyclades in 1971.

The network set up by ARPA, known as the ARPANET, allowed scientific research institutions and military research centers across the US to be connected to each other. In the 1960s, information (data) and computer programs (software) had to be moved from one device to another, with data often stored on physical punch cards or with large computer tapes. Researchers had difficulty accessing computers unless there was one close to them. Moving information around by plane was arduous. Even when scientists went to work at a computer elsewhere, there were queues to run programs, and the programmers had to wait their turn. Ensuring efficient use of the computers was critical. As a result, dedicated data telephone lines were purchased, for connections of major computing centers to each other. Connecting computers so that programs and data could move quickly and cost-efficiently was thus very valuable. One day, to move programs, someone at SRI invented a way to have short messages and attach accompanying programs or data. This little digital message, moving from one computer to another, was arguably the first email.

Bill Gates as a teenager was deeply engaged with these computers. As a very talented teenage programmer, he was writing innovative software to carry out computationally heavy calculations, largely at night. At the time, computers were then shared by multiple people, with large applications typically running at night. If a computer bug forced a computer to restart, everyone lost their work for that night. Therefore, the scarcity of computing capacity became an important constraint on the pace of technological progress. One of Bill Gates' programs calculated the optimal timing of streetlights in Seattle so that during rush hours, and other times, traffic could move smoothly. This apparently simple problem entailed complex calculations. Bill Gates and his friends, like all talented programmers, would sometimes have bugs in their program that could crash a computer and require it to be rebooted. This experience forced him to optimize his code writing to limit errors and was a reason he became an acknowledged brilliant programmer.

Bill Gates developed his early computer programming prowess partly on government subsidized computing equipment. This equipment had, essentially, been put in place for developing innovative new technologies that could serve purposes like supporting the local Seattle aerospace powerhouse, Boeing, with its need for aerospace designs both for military and civilian use.

The military-industrial complex ultimately realized that two things were critical with computers: the ability to move information from one place to another and the resilience to ensure that an attack in one place could not wipe out critical information capabilities. Much of this thinking was driven by the Cold War and the worries about the impact of targeted nuclear strikes. The question was how to maintain computing capabilities after a hostile event or other localized breakdown, and in particular the ability to communicate and exchange information after such strikes.

The internet protocols allowed computer messages to pass from one transfer point (or "node") to another on the way to their final destination. The existence of multiple potential paths between two computers makes the entire system resistant to enemy attacks on one location, or even multiple locations, allowing the continued transfer of information from one large computing center to another.

This decentralized web of communications can automatically reconfigure how they sent information from one place to another. That means that if Seattle and Washington wanted to communicate, and there were three routes by which information moved (e.g., via Chicago, St Louis or satellite), even if the Chicago and satellite links were knocked out, as people feared during the cold war, from a nuclear strikes and a satellite attack, communications would automatically reconfigure to travel via St Louis.

In fact, the web of connections envisioned to protect from large scale nuclear war required many more connections than three, much like an interconnected web.

The decentralized structure of the Internet was never designed to prevent government control. It was not an anarchist effort to take power for the people. Rather, emerging from a research institute need, the web became a conscious US government effort to create a strong and unbreakable system of transmitting information, even in the worst disaster scenarios.

The points to draw from this are that the internet infrastructure grew out of US government efforts to create a communications infrastructure resistant to wars. The US government long perceived controlling the development of the Internet as part of its normal role to ensure that the United States would remain fully operational in case war came to its shores, an occurrence from which it had been largely spared during its life as a nation, once independence was achieved.

The US government owned or funded the initial infrastructure. Computer science researchers were not in league with the government. But they undoubtedly recognized the key role played by the financial support of the US government in making these technological revolutions possible. Consequently, they knew the rules they had to play by. The US government has always kept a strong control and influence over the Internet.

France, meanwhile, where many of the key concepts underlying the internet protocol originated, largely failed in the mass commercialization of their technology. In the early 1980s its national telecom company, France Télécom, developed a revolutionary technology at the time, the Minitel. The computer-like device gave its users access to many services such as weather information, stock prices, train reservations and access to a nationwide phone directory. Its birth was largely the result of a desire of the French government to ensure the country's technological leadership and independence. Despite its tremendous success in France, it did not achieve any substantial cross-border distribution. This was not for lack of trying. Sales and product releases were made in multiple countries, from Belgium's release via Belgacom to Germany's Bildschirmtext, Spain's Ibertex which reached 275,000 installations in 1991, the Netherlands with Viditel and Videotex, South Africa's Beltel and Canada's Alex, in addition to a test with Qwest in Minneapolis and Omaha. These systems were operated over proprietary networks. In France, France Télécom succeeded to slow the introduction of the open protocol, largely due to the perceived threat to their preferred operational mode of a closed system and the wide availability of the closed system alternative. While the French Minitel helped French brick-and-mortar businesses to be ready for the world wide web, the French would not lead in Internet adoption, due to the prior commitment to a closed and constrained interface delivered by the incumbent telecom operator. The unquestionable French lead in mass release of digital technology was squandered by the country and is an example of a missed opportunity.

Similarly, Japan had advanced experience in home computing posts by 1972, when it had 130,000 posts with keyboards in Osaka and Tokyo. 60 percent of these had access to a network under the Ministry of Telecommunications containing a library of scientific information. This Japanese lead was also squandered, again because of a commitment to a closed interface.

Today, the Internet has evolved in ways that were largely unpredictable in 1970. The key breaking point was the introduction of the protocol that allowed files to be called up directly from another computer connected on the public network. While databases and other files had been callable for some time, creating a way to open distant files and to name places where they are stored in a way that all intermediate "nodes" would understand and be able to pass on the information was revolutionary. This Internet protocol existed for more than 20 years before the "http" overlay laid the foundation for the first mass browser, launched in 1993 as Mosaic and developed by Marc Andreesen while a student at the University of Illinois. This browser then transformed into Netscape under the company of the same name in Silicon Valley. This product became the first mass browser.

The advantages of other countries were lost, in large part, following the development of a choice for users between open and closed systems. The Minitel and its international relatives were closed systems, in which sites had to be approved by a central authority and whose operators could effectively run an online shopping mall that they controlled. Like the Minitel, the main Internet access for most Americans in the late 1990s, AOL, was a closed system at its origin. The US worldwide internet dominance might never have occurred if AOL had maintained its sway over users. After years of trying to maintain a proprietary interface, and after having lost about half of its subscribers, AOL completely changed its business model away from a "walled garden" model to a free model, building on its established subscriber base of 12-13 million users with its August 2006 switch to providing email accounts to non-paying subscribers, symbolizing their recognition that open systems were the future.

Meanwhile, the Minitel declined slowly but surely, until it was quietly unplugged in 2012. But it should not be forgotten that the advantage on implementing a publicly networked systems that brings together customers and companies initially rested with France. The French lost this advantage by not adapting quickly enough to consumer demands and by giving system control to a single incumbent telecommunications company.

Silicon Valley has figured out how to make such adaptations, how to combine human resources with funding and how to invest for a long-term return. The Silicon Valley search for "home runs," which are epitomized by Google (Alphabet), Amazon, Apple, Intel and Facebook (Meta), has been bearing fruit for decades. This fruit is now gloriously ripe. The ability of a business model to quickly scale and go across borders is created by the very structure of the Internet, the structure that was initially controlled by and developed for the US government military-industrial complex. In another sense, this has been a great gift to the world, taking it forward and creating new ways for consumers and businesses to interact. In another sense, this has been an international takeover like no other.

In the US search engine market, Google has about 70 percent market share, while in Europe, their share is 90 percent or more. From a consumer perspective, search provides the ability to learn and discover in ways never previously imagined. You want to know the name and height of the tallest mountain in Scotland? It is Ben Nevis, with a height of 4,413 feet. You want to know where Evian water comes from? The town of Evian, in France. You want to know who designed the Empire State Building? William Lamb. Easy.

Searches like these help Google to understand your interests. In fact, employees of Google boast that they can predict your actions and likes better than a spouse.

Then when you search for holidays, Google may know that you are interested in hiking and environmentally friendly places, that you dream of a cruise ship to Norway or that you like to go to beaches or go skiing. It may match your holiday searches with appropriately places to go and stay, given your interests. At the same time, it may use what can be thought of almost as sub-contractors to complete the search, such as Booking.com or Expedia. Google can connect you with a seller of chairs, and Amazon may come out at the top of such a search. The search activity is fundamental to all purchases. Businesses need ways to reach consumers. Advertising in traditional media used to be the main method. Increasingly paying for search results is taking over, as well as showing up in so-called "natural" results of search engines, which are those the search engine chooses to show without receiving any compensation.

Google sells businesses the opportunity to appear high up in search results, with a tiny marker "Ad" in English to indicate that the business paid for a result. When customers click through to the link, Google is usually paid for that click by the advertiser.

Google has the opportunity to learn demands and willingness to pay of individual consumers, to know costs of suppliers, and to seek to appropriate third-party profits and consumer surplus for itself. For this to succeed, it needs that there be competitors to Amazon and Booking.com who are willing to bid up the price of search result placement. This competition ensures that Google receives the main profit from search.

For repeat purchases, Google may not have a significant role to play, so the customer surplus on repeat purchases may go to the intermediaries who have "acquired" the customer.

What this means for small and medium sized businesses is that they will increasingly lose the ability to maintain their markups for themselves. Markups may rise generally, to cover the increased ability to charge customers close to their maximum willingness to pay.

The irony for this is that the Internet, which was initially thought to reduce consumer difficulty of finding goods and reduce search costs, has instead created a mechanism for customizing prices to consumers and sucking surplus profits out of established business. This is happening not just in the

US, but more generally worldwide. Google is generating net income of $76 billion, with a market capitalization of $1.6 trillion. Facebook (Meta), which is the other main advertising behemoth, has a net income of $39.4 billion and market capitalization of $635 billion. Jointly with the other top 6 digital companies, they are worth more than the entire capitalization of the US stock market in the year 1999.

The US government has maintained significant control over the Internet, despite the international ubiquity of the service. For example, the .com domain names have been assigned by companies under the oversight of the US Department of Commerce. More broadly, the US government retained exclusive control over the Internet Corporation for Assigned Names and Numbers until deciding to relinquish full control, as announced in 2014. During most of the development of the Internet, the US government retained an unparalleled ability to influence structure of the Internet and to observe traffic over the Internet.

Companies like Google, Microsoft and others are regularly put under secret legal obligation to provide information to the US Government. These demands typically arise from legislation that gives the right to the government to make demands on companies in the interests of national security, and the companies have no right to appeal such demands, nor even the right to make publicly known the nature of the demands that are made. The national security orders that can be delivered by the Foreign Intelligence Surveillance Court had been kept under a broad veil of secrecy until disclosures about the PRISM program of US government gathering of information by former National Security Agency analyst Edward Snowden. After companies were permitted to reveal aggregate information, it emerged that government orders to Google had increased from about 2000 in 2009 to 12-13,000 in 2012, with Microsoft's peaking at 16-17,000 in 2012. More recently, AT&T received demands for information on 14,500-14,999 customers under the Foreign Intelligence Surveillance Act in Jan-June 2021 and 2,000-2,499 customers via National Security "letters". Out of the total of more than 270 million customers, these numbers are arguably relatively modest, but the collection of information from these people may involve further collection of information on their contacts, substantially expanding the number of people impacted by such orders.

These demands are not the only way that the US Government is obtaining information on internet usage.

In an anonymous looking building in San Francisco, the trans-Pacific optical cable wires mount into a massive telecommunications distribution network historically run by AT&T. One of the floors on this building is not controlled by AT&T, however. It is instead run by a US government agency according to a reputed documentary program on US public television, Frontline. A reasonable presumption is that the US Government is intercepting all the incoming and outgoing traffic from this transatlantic cable, part of the massive "listening" program effectively revealed by Edward Snowden.

The government even now could be presumed to take advantage of back doors to access information in other countries, just as other countries have sought to do with US information. Some of the substantial software and hardware flaws that are discovered are not disclosed in ways one would imagine. In 2017 Google notified Intel, then Microsoft and Amazon, of a major flaw that left computers with Intel and ARM chips susceptible to "Meltdown" and "Spectre" attacks. These attacks could have let intruders access logins and other information at different security layers of computers. The flaw was one of the most serious backdoor problems known. While this was one of the largest holes ever discovered, Google allegedly did not inform the US government, instead preferring to use NDAs with relevant affected parties itself. One reason could have been to prevent the US government from exploiting the flaw.

The NSA is rumored to have paid $10 million to RSA, the maker of widely used security encryption technology, to change a feature in its encryption software. One hypothesis would be that the change would make encryption easier for the NSA to break encryption. This could demonstrate one part of US government influence on basic internet security. But there can be other ways in which the US government exercises its control over US companies.

In part for security reasons, but also for commercial ones, the Chinese government has limited Google's operations in China. One reason may be Google can be required on the decision of one anonymous judge from Washington to turn over reams of information to the US security apparatus.

Other countries have not been as careful as China. Consequently, Google has assembled the most detailed private mapping information of geography and buildings in the world.

Pokémon Go is an internet game that has collected astonishing additional geographic information on top of Google's. Founded by a former Google staffer, Pokémon Go places cartoon characters in real world locations using mobile phones. Players of the game will know that they capture characters at public locations. Of more concern, the game has incentivized players to provide photos, via snapshots and "photobombing," that can include private interiors. In return, players can get access to special and rare characters (such as one called the "Smeargle.") The company can thus collect extensive details of internal home layouts, often provided by children without parental authorization.

The ubiquity of the Internet and GPS mapping seems to have made systematic mapping of the streets of the world by Google an unremarkable event. Yet in previous epochs, detailed maps were regarded as confidential material. As a result, countries seldom allowed foreigners to conduct detailed mapping exercises within their own borders. Satellite images at a high detail were considered top-secret resources. Yet Google has done exactly what would have been unthinkable for a government, running up and down the streets of countries around the world with sophisticated camera and electronic equipment. It even identified the exact locations of different modem boxes and thus could identify exactly the source of most internet activity. When Google "accidentally" simultaneously collected information on the simultaneous internet activity of these boxes in France, that was considered a violation of privacy. Yet the information is separately available to Google through its google analytics software collection that is spread deeply on the Internet and almost unavoidable.

Google is serving as the primary access point to information, much as US oil refiners in 1900 served as the primary access point to oil products. Then, if you drew oil from the soil, you had to process that through a trust of refiners who were acting as one. Then, if you wanted to buy oil products, you had to do so through the refiners. They had a monopoly. Google is not very different, and the idea of market power is long established in economics. By serving as the unique access point to search for many people, Google has an enormous power to influence the course of economic transactions and even to influence the way that people think about the world.

In a remarkable commercial arrangement, when Google contracts with websites to place display ads, the default contract with those companies does not specify a specific formula for payment. Apart from content publishers receiving 68 percent and search publishers receiving 51 percent, Google says they "do not disclose the revenue share for other AdSense products". Until 2010, not even the average revenue splits between Google and content providers using AdSense were known. In short, the providers of advertising space to Google have sometimes acted like workers reimbursed only at the will of the master.

As we know, Google subtly includes ads at the top of search results. They position ads at the top because many people will click on the first options presented to them, instead of clicking below at the natural or "true" search results. Occasionally they now place ads at the bottom of a page and may place more than the old maximum of three ads. Obviously, this system is much more profitable to Google than its old habit of placing ads to the side or bottom of search results. Consumer protection agencies are doing little to protect consumers from this potential fraud, considering that the very small notice saying "Ad" is sufficient to inform consumers that they are receiving an advertisement. Many companies are willing to pay for these ads even when they are the number one natural search result. Indeed, if they do not do so, another company may take out an ad on their search words, which will mean that they would no longer be at the top of search results.

Apple is succeeding in gaining revenue from many sources, such as games, music and material sold over its unique platforms. They can charge a high percentage of revenues (often 30 percent) for a very low-cost service, due to their absolute control over the market for apps on their devices thanks to the Appstore. Given that consumers have no choice, once locked into an Apple product, Apple gains monopoly power over access to the consumers using its operating systems.

Google is doing the same with Android, though with a more permissive entry system onto its applications platform, and a much wider distribution of phones. In the long run, most apps will be distributed over its platform.

Amazon is a different type of company. Money losing over most of its life, it has operated with razor-thin margins for its average product portfolio, while expanding its vision of widespread direct delivery services to people. Via user decisions, it has nonetheless the effect of putting some local businesses out of operation, such as bookstores, via its superior product breadth and remarkably capable distribution mechanisms. Online ordering leads to many more delivery trips balanced by fewer customer shopping expeditions.

Amazon's international success has been astounding. Its algorithm enables it to make automated reading recommendations that are difficult for bookstores to duplicate without knowing the purchase history of a client. While in individual markets overseas, book chains have sought to compete for online sales with Amazon, they have been unable to do so with equal success. Google though could compete for book sales. Perhaps in knowledge of this, Amazon pays Google for search. If Amazon did not pay for these ads, customers could move in droves to other options suggested by Google, most potentially itself. This possibility can push even Amazon to pay Google closer to the marginal profitability that it derives from its customers. While Amazon maintains a marketplace that often offers good deals and prices to customers, system factors that raise its costs are likely to be passed on, ultimately, to consumers. In effect, by focusing on search, Google can mop up consumer surplus from consumers and other internet giants.

Travel reservations have been one of the largest sources of revenue for Google, coming not only from flight reservation systems, Booking.com and Expedia, but also from airlines and hotel companies. The reason that these are good sources of revenue is the same as that which permitted American Express to charge higher commission to hotels and restaurants than stores. The hotels and restaurants are battling with each other to fill their excess capacity. Every customer who books an empty room for more than it costs to clean it yields a positive cash flow for the hotel. But a positive cash flow from a series of stays does not mean that a hotel will reimburse its cost of construction. Much of the gain from these investments now goes to online booking platforms.

The margins of online travel agencies can vary from 15 to 25 percent. American-owned entities are suddenly taking a margin from the travel industry worldwide. Hotels around the world pay these entities for referrals. Similarly, TripAdvisor, which gives the impression of being a neutral arbiter of quality to consumers, has tripled some of the fees it charges to hotels simply to list their website in 2016 and 2017. TripAdvisor has realized that it serves a function much like Google in general search. It is a specialized search company and, in some cases, may be able to earn between $1 and perhaps up to $10 for every review left, depending on the place reviewed, information that is not shared with those who write their reviews for free.

The supposed benefits to companies and consumers from reducing search costs is not being realized. In fact, there is some reason to believe that the new structure of industry, with search intermediaries dominating sales channels for hotels, and increasingly for restaurants, is leading to both higher prices for consumers and, ironically, lower profits for the hotels and restaurants, as they pay out enormous percentages of their revenues for commissions. These are not markets where competition is working well. These are markets where the Internet has perverted competition and has done so to the benefit of US companies. The consequent economic value resounds disproportionately to the US, in terms of corporate profits, taxes, and salaries. This is one of the reasons that the US government sees the open Internet, with free cross-border trade, as tremendously advantageous to the United States. However, in this zero-sum game, what is advantageous to the United States is detrimental to other countries. Their economies, and especially the margins in their domestic businesses, are being taken over by US companies.

Sneaking up on us day by day, the international dimension of the takeover is astonishing.

3. A TRUE TAKEOVER

He that is master of the sea may, in some sort, be said to be Master of every country; at least such as are bordering on the sea. For he is at liberty to begin and end War, where, when and on what terms he please, and extend his conquests even to the Antipodes.
-Joseph Gander

The extent of the Internet takeover can be illustrated across many different domains of economic activity.

In hotels, more than 51 percent of US hotel reservations in 2018 came to hotels indirectly over third-party reservation sites. These systems charge hotels about 15 to 30 percent of their sales revenues, potentially raising costs to customers.

In bookselling, online outlets have increased their share of book sales compared to brick-and-mortar ones. There are major advantages to Amazon, such as its choice being up to 23 times larger than a book superstore, with 30-40 percent of its sold books being ones that are not available in brick-and-mortar stores. As many as one half of local independent bookstores have closed between 2000 and 2020, with the US having experienced a 50% decline in the number of bookstores between 1998 and 2019 according to US Census data, from 12,151 to 6,045. The number of bookstores has also been divided by two in the UK, with only 967 still in business in 2021 according to Companies House. France has lost 27 percent of its Paris region bookstores between 2002 and 2020 according to Les Echos. Germany lost more than 1,250 bookstores out of more than 6,200 over the six-year period between 2011 and 2017. While part of these declines in bookstore presence could be due to mismanagement at the bookstore level, many booksellers suggest that online book sales, ebook sales and reduced reading activity may be behind these changes.

In film, movies are now sold, rented or viewed over the Internet more than ever before; though cinema is still strong, with a record $41 billion in ticket sales in 2018. Online streaming services have offered consumers a large choice of movies and series that they can watch from the comfort of their own home. While we have lost the mass video store chain, in many respects we are better off. But in terms of competition, we are not. Movie resources for streaming are divided between major streaming services like Netflix, Disney+, Prime and Hulu. If you want to watch films and series made by Netflix, you need a Netflix subscription. Most streaming platforms do not allow customers to purchase or rent films piece by piece. Instead, when you subscribe, you receive a bundle, including films that you do not want. The carve-up of video resources, matched with a take-all-or-leave-it business model, forces people to subscribe to multiple platforms. For example, if a Netflix user wants a Disney+ film, they must sign up to Disney+ for a month. The bundling and non-overlapping options push up customer expenditure on movies and TV series.

For those who are seeking to buy a given major studio film at a cheap price over the Internet, good luck. The choice is surprisingly restricted.

Before internet film distribution took off, the predominant format was DVD. People who were done with a DVD would place it into the secondhand market. The choice of places to buy secondhand DVDs was enormous and prices varied substantially. This broad secondhand market choice created a pressure on sellers of new DVDs to keep prices reasonable. New DVDs were often available in multibuy offers grouped with other DVDs.

Prior to the internet revolution, secondhand DVDs placed some constraint on the price that could be charged for a new one. While secondhand DVDs could sometimes be purchased for as little as $0.50, finding a movie purchase over the Internet for less than $9.00 is challenging.

The pressure on sellers that existed from having so many options for purchasing a DVD has vanished with the rise of the streaming services. The competition has been destroyed by the technological capability to restrict the number of devices on which films are viewed, and to ensure that only the authorized original purchaser on a device can use the service. Effectively, the movement from DVD to internet video has raised the cost of specific individual films for those who are cost conscious. As the competition from secondhand versions of old movies disappears, the price of old movies remains close to the original price of a newly released film. These developments are great for Hollywood and all the new gatekeepers to film watching, like Apple. There is one group for whom the reduction in options is not so good: us. The cost increase is not trivial for those of us want affordable ways to watch movies. For the illustrative prices cited here, the increase is 1800 percent.

For restaurants, the role of the Internet in customer interaction has expanded dramatically with the rise of food delivery from platform intermediaries and of online booking through internet intermediaries. Do you know what happens when you order a meal over the Internet? In addition to us paying a delivery fee, the restaurant has to pay a substantial fee, which can be equivalent to 15 percent of the cost of the meal, to the intermediary. This additional cost to the restaurant is then in large part borne by us. Is the small increase in convenience worth that much? As more people use these intermediaries, a restaurant operating at close to its cost is forced to raise its prices. Many restaurants feel that they do not have a choice about whether to participate in the schemes. Each restaurant faces a classic problem: their individual dominant strategy is to list themselves on the restaurant booking or rating apps, even if as a group they are financially worse off.

We are increasingly choosing ride-hailing services over traditional taxis. There are many good reasons to do this, including that ride hailers have direct knowledge of who their drivers are. In Mexico, occasional kidnappings in officially registered taxis led Mexicans with smartphones to prefer ride hailing services. The prices are reasonable, but even more important, if they are kidnapped, there is a way for the police to track down their kidnapper. This is a great improvement over traditional taxi service. As ride hailing companies have expanded, they have created fantastic new opportunities for travelers. They have also broken the stranglehold of a profession that was largely overprotected, the taxi license owner.

Nonetheless, abusive practices are generalized and have so far rarely been prosecuted. For example, ride hailing companies argue that their drivers are independent contractors, yet they are alleged to sometimes push their drivers not to work for competitors. Unlike for a typical contractor, ride hailing services do not always even tell their drivers how much they will be paid for each ride. Instead, some give the driver a pay packet at the end of the day and over time may add various bonuses to that, some of which may arrive a year later.

From the customer perspective, ride hailers regularly engage in low balling the estimated arrival time of a driver. In particular, at busy rush hours, a ride-hailer's estimated 10-minute wait for a car in Mexico City often, was, at least in my experience, an underestimate by at least 20 minutes; it never took less than the estimated time. Are ride-hailing companies preying on our optimism that keeps us stuck with drivers who will not come on time in order to prevent us trying a competitor? Maybe. Yet they can punish riders for cancelling a ride even if they have misled us to think it would come much earlier than it did. Fairness is not part of the equation.

If ride-hailing companies are smart, they will ultimately price discriminate between different people for the same route. One major company says that users are more likely to pay for surge pricing when their phone batteries are low. In the future, the companies could use location data to identify those who live or work in areas with substantial income to charge them higher rates. This is the ultimate objective of the internet companies: to extract the consumer surplus that is available, as much as possible, while keeping customers happy with each client purchase. Taxi drivers operating with regulated fare schemes cannot extract this surplus.

Price increases do not only apply at the sector-specific level. Apple and Google have been obtaining 30 percent commissions on sales made over their application interfaces. App makers quite reasonably respond to these charging mechanisms, if they can, by reducing the purchasing options available to us over apps. The Kindle App from Apple's App Store does not show the possibility to buy e-books from the Kindle store, because Amazon prefers its customers to buy on platforms where it would not have to pay this hefty commission. Thus, in order to add books to their Kindle, users need to use an Amazon website. Amazon thus protects its users from paying higher costs due to the Apple commission structure. In contrast, when you subscribe to Prime Video over the Apple Prime Video App, some observers believe that Apple takes a commission of possibly 30 percent in the first year and 15 percent in subsequent years. If that is right, guess whose pockets are emptied to pay for these hidden commissions of 30 percent? Consumers and app businesses are paying. With Apple doing nothing to invest in the raw material (e.g., by making films) they are reaping gains from their gatekeeping stranglehold over access to their devices.

While we know platforms are charging for their services, we have no idea of the extent of those charges. Milestones in government understanding include major independent expert reports like the Crémer-Montjoye-Schweitzer report for the European Commission, the Furman Review for the UK government and the US-focused Stigler Center review authored by Scott Morton and others. These reports from 2019 describe possible mechanisms of competitive harm from internet business models, like creating moats to protect core businesses, buying competitors, and abusing market power. What they do not emphasize is that, in aggregate, the cost impacts can so large that they are likely leading to higher prices for many products and reduce purchasing power overall. The irony is that this is not truly inherent to the Internet but arises from the consumer's own choices.

One of the important consumer choices is over which search engine to use. In 2021 Google was used in 92 percent of searches in Europe. In the US it accounts for between 70 and 80 percent of the market share. The growth in online search and, more generally, online advertising, has been accompanied by a shrinkage in traditional media spending. Declining spending has an impact on amount of traditional news and magazine reading produced and, sometimes, on quality.

The revenues of news outlets have fallen dramatically. Between 2007 and 2020, newspaper and magazine ad revenue has fallen from around $125 billion in 2007 down to about $30 billion in 2020 according to the advertising tracker WARC. As of 2020, search and social media ad spend jointly exceed television ad spend. When news content leads to advertising over Google, the question arises of how much is passed on to news outlets. India's Digital News Publishers

Association claims that Google only gives publishers 10-15 percent of the revenue earned from their news websites and that 50 percent of traffic comes from Google, 25-30 percent from social media, and only 10-15 percent coming directly.

In one remarkable experiment, Google ceased to show traditional news outlets in its searches in Spain in 2014, in response to a legislative initiative that would have prevented it from continuing to profit from these sources as it had previously done. Google repeated the exercise in Australia, again in response to governmental threats. The contention of the Australian authorities was that while Google needed news outlets, it did not need any individual outlet, which gave it disproportionate bargaining power.

While we do not know all the impacts of these experiments, one thing is sure: the news companies were paying close attention. And when Google takes their revenue, that reduces the revenue for investing to make quality news on which society depends for reliable public information and educating the electorate about current affairs.

The stock valuation of the large internet companies has grown to extraordinary levels. Of course, stock values will change over time and with market developments. But to give a sense of magnitude, as of April 2022, Alphabet, the owner of Google, was worth, $1.76 trillion, Alibaba from China $286 billion, Amazon $1.57 trillion, and Apple $2.7 trillion, Meta (Facebook) $635 billion, Microsoft $2.2 trillion, and Tencent from China $453 billion. These are only some of the more well-known success stories. Overall, internet companies have a stock valuation of at least $7.4 trillion as categorized by companiesmarketcap.com. This number does not even account for Apple and Microsoft due to their non-internet activities. The overall figure exceeds that of the oil industry, steel industry and car industry combined. If we include Apple and Microsoft as part of the digital grouping, the digital companies account for about 10 percent of total market capitalizations of companies of $91.8 trillion. How can this possibly be? The main answer is that their expected future earnings have risen remarkably.

Moreover, the internet companies' aggregate valuation is, at least for the moment, much higher than one of the most popular digital topics in the news, cryptocurrencies. The internet company valuation dwarfs Bitcoin and other virtual currencies. Bitcoins, perhaps the most extraordinary story of a virtual asset gaining value as a tradable commodity, increased in value from $3 to $53,000 between 2013 and 2022, fueling the creation of a broader cryptocurrency asset class that reached a book value under $1 trillion according to Pitchbook. This total value is less than 5 percent of the value of the internet companies as whole.

The ownership nationality of the top internet companies creates concerns outside of the US and China. Out of the top 10 internet companies, *all* are based in the US or China. These companies are, in decreasing order of valuation, Alphabet, Amazon, Meta, Tencent, Alibaba, Netflix, PayPal, Meituan, Airbnb and ServiceNow. Out of the top 20 internet companies, 17 are based in the US or China and *none* in Europe. In fact, the first "European" company to enter the list is Spotify, at position 38, and the next one is Zalando at position 55. Not only are the top European internet companies low on the global ladder, but their ownership is not solely European, especially in the case of Spotify. The lack of more European members of the top league of internet companies is a perplexing problem from the perspective of European governments. The lack of developing country companies is similarly a problem from the perspective of their governments.

The story of unicorns born in Europe is also much less telling. Many companies *were* created in Europe or included European founders, such as Skype, Spotify, BlaBlaCar, Booking.com, Deezer, YouTube, and WhatsApp. These are among the most successful digital enterprises born in

Europe. How many remain in European hands? Arguably, only BlaBlaCar and Deezer are majority owned by Europeans, and these two are those with the lowest market capitalizations of the list of companies with European founders. All the other companies have been bought by American ones. Their streams of profits have been increased multi-fold and moved over to the US, benefitting primarily US stockholders and the US corporate tax purse. While top internet companies have been bought by American ones, top American companies have not equally been bought by Europeans. The Americans here showed their dual talents in financial engineering and strategic focus on acquisition. This asymmetry means that the ownership of the key successful internet companies in the world has increasingly been pushed towards a heavyweight influence of the US. Where organic growth of US companies is not sufficient, Americans simply buy the top technology and then market it themselves to grow it to its potential.

The exception to US dominance is within China where homegrown internet giants have emerged. These companies grew largely because the Chinese government prevented foreign companies from pushing out local ones and prevented foreign acquisition of its companies. But the Chinese internet giants also grew in part because of their remarkable ability to learn from successful foreign companies and then to innovate.

Attempts by European governments to stop acquisitions by foreigners create a politically hazy realm of political interference in deals without clear rules. If foreign deals are to be stopped, clear rules are needed. But rather than trying to interfere with matters of corporate control and ownership, it would be much easier to tackle the issue of the taxation of profits. Otherwise, the internet-induced downfall of local tax-paying brick-and-mortar companies in favor of foreign-owned internet companies paying taxes abroad will worsen the budget deficit of the losers of the internet war.

Local taxes on internet profits have historically been avoided by the leading internet companies According to the OECD's Base Erosion and Profit Shifting action plan, approved by G20 ministers in September 2013, the location of the profits should be aligned with the location of the activity. In practice, according to the OECD's tax group leader Pascal Saint-Amans, this would mean that the location of a company's production should determine the recipient country of profit taxation. Given the predominant weight of American production for digital companies, this means that taxes on profits generated by internet companies are being paid primarily in the United States. Up until now, the amount paid in tax by internet companies, and other companies, is visible through corporate reports only in an aggregate form across all countries. Tax payments are not generally transparent at the level of individual countries. European governments may feel though that dramatically little has been paid, in profit taxes, to the European countries whose customers could account for as much as one third to one half of sales. If western sales (and profits) are distributed in proportion to national GDP, considering how much has been paid in the US, much larger tax amounts should have been paid in Europe.

In response to the concerns that large companies are obtaining sweetheart tax deals in some countries of the European Union, the European Commission investigated several companies, including Amazon and Apple from 2014 to 2017. It concluded that Apple had received about 13 billion Euros in improper state approved tax reductions in Ireland and Amazon 250 million Euros in Luxembourg. These decisions were among a series of European Commission findings on government subsidies via improper tax deals that appeared particularly focused on US internet companies. While the decisions show a will for action, the European Commission efforts are failing, as its administrative decisions have been struck down by the

European Union's General Court in 2020 for Apple and 2021 for Amazon.

While preferential tax treatment has been alleged to help US internet companies in their competition overseas, a much more fundamental source of their success has been their capacity at building up raw market power. Internet companies that serve as intermediaries, and that do not face substantial competition, obtain the unilateral power to raise prices. As an illustration of market power in action, it is crucial to understand the multi-sided pricing model of intermediary platforms.

Google provides many services for free to consumers, such as search capabilities. It then charges online merchants which use its advertising service for redirecting consumers to their websites. Google earns revenue from clicks on these paid-for search results, which appear on top of the search result page, but does not directly make money from clicks on normal "organic" answers. As a result, Google's core financial incentive is to make people click on the ads.

In its early days, Yahoo and Google clearly distinguished their ads and put them in separate boxes. This was much less profitable for Google than other means of reaching customers, such as mixing ads in a list of search results. Today, the ads shown in search results are not distinguished with a bold and vibrant color from other search results. This failure to blatantly distinguish ads from other content is arguably misleading for many ordinary users who, if not paying close attention, may sometimes click on an ad thinking it is a normal result. If these presentations of ads constitute, misleading representations about advertising, they are arguably illegal. Yet prosecutions against Google for misrepresentation have been few, in part because Google always maintains a notice, however small and difficult to read, that distinguish ads from other search results.

By charging nothing for search enquiries to users like us, and by delivering a good quality of results, Google obtains substantial loyalty from users who make searches, whether the users have multiple search engines or not. On a given device, most consumers would make their searches over one search engine. Google's is by far the most common. So when you search for a secondhand original Mini Cooper, advertisers are more likely to reach you over Google, not Yahoo.

A possible consequence of this market power on search is that Google is able to charge up to 30 to 40 percent more for an advertising click as alternative services, according to the UK's Competition and Markets Authority.

Ironically, Google has no direct financial incentive to help consumers find good deals. It actually can have an incentive to place them into worse deals. For example, if you search for "cheap car insurance," how will Google make the most money from this search? It is not through helping you to find a service with a low margin. Instead, it would be through steering you to a service that would have a high markup which, in turn, could afford to pay for higher advertising fees to Google.

Google simply exemplifies the practice of many other sector-specific services. TripAdvisor, for example, has an excellent user-based review service for restaurants and hotels and other activities. However, you will notice that for many hotels, they advertise rooms for sale with an online travel agency, like Booking.com. Unless hotels pay to have their websites linked, the link to the hotel and phone number for direct contact would not exist. Thus, even though many consumers would like to contact hotels directly, the system is setup through one intermediary to lead to another intermediary. The fees that hotels pay for TripAdvisor services have in many cases tripled or quadrupled in recent years.

Yet there is a real policy question as to whether TripAdvisor should even be able to charge hotels or restaurants for listing their contact information. The fact they can do so does not give them the right to extract value from a trademarked name, which is exactly what they and the online travel agencies are often doing.

While you might know that restaurant delivery services earn a commission when you use their services, you might not be aware that TripAdvisor, restaurant booking companies or delivery services also earn money from restaurants through its platform. All this results in increased costs for restaurants, which they are willing to pay only because their competitor restaurants do so as well. But what is the ultimate impact of this on users? The answer is disturbing, but obvious. When variable costs for a service are raised, prices for the service will (almost) inevitably be raised as well, though not necessarily by the same amount. The intermediaries typically demand that the commissions be taken from the retail prices. Their commission will then be averaged into the price for all customers. Remarkably, we the users are almost never told the true size of commissions; the platforms do not want us to know their size. The sellers in turn are afraid of being banned or punished by the platforms, and are contractually forbidden to suggest we reserve directly. The result is a distortion of information and competition that can hurt both consumers and advertisers.

People who do not use the internet services have to pay more for their food as a result of the large portion of people who are increasingly using internet food-ordering services.

If this sounds like a system of institutionalized taking of money from one group of customers to support the higher costs of another, perhaps it is. The internet-using customers distort the predominant price constraining mechanism. The typical mechanism is that stores keep prices reasonable to attract the marginal customers, who are interested in low prices. In this case, the internet searchers may both be the customers most willing to move to another provider, and in this sense marginal, but be raising prices for others.

As the guard Marcellus said in Shakespeare's *Hamlet*,

"Something smells rotten in the state of Denmark." And it is not cheese. Nor is the smell limited to Denmark. The smell is the combination of the inadequacy of many governments' own tax systems, and certain cases of exploitation of market power. On the one hand, it is the market power exercised by internet platforms which contributes to their very high earnings. On the other hand, it is the trivial payments of corporate or general taxes on these sales in most countries where multinational digital companies operate. These low taxes are *not* a problem with the companies themselves and are *not* tax evasion. Instead, the low taxes arise directly from government failures with their own taxation mechanisms.

The standard of taxation of profits in the country of corporate headquarters can be seen as a modern form of vassal or colonial exploitation. The number one colonial power of the digital world would then be viewed as the United States.

This colonial power has been obtained by peaceful means, but the final economic effects resemble those from the historic expansions of territory by war.

An Internet Empire has been constructed from a new type of war. While its means of territorial takeover have been different from violent wars, its hard economic logic has been the same as in much of the empire building over the course of history.

4. ECONOMIC GAIN AS A PURPOSE OF WAR

Endless money forms the sinews of war.
    -Cicero

Historically, one of the primary purposes of war is to obtain economic benefit for the attacker. According to Clausewitz, the well-known Prussian commentator on war, war is conceived as simply an extension of diplomacy, and is about improving the situation of the country that starts the war.

Many wars and empires have had a purpose to create economic gain for the victors. While this purpose does not change over time, the methods of achieving economic control have evolved. While traditional terrestrial wars based on armed conflict and military engagement continue to be fought for the control of land, digital companies illustrate a new method for achieving many of the economic objectives of war. Control over the digital economy can be viewed as a modernized extension of war, one that, in practice, operates to the ultimate benefit of a new American empire.

To demonstrate the point that economic gain has often been a purpose of war, we examine the role of economic gain in many previous extensions of territorial control. Empires that do not create sufficient new revenue and extra gains from territorial expansion will quickly fail. In contrast, those empires that have succeeded in their expansion did so by creating sufficient extra economic activity and wealth to cover the costs of empire expansion (including armies and costs of occupation.)

In short, a "rational" war would proceed when an aggressor's financial expectations of gain exceed the expected cost to take control of their rival's resources. The territorial growth occurs as long as it is profitable to the central state to have such growth and for the central state to take direct military control or indirect client-state control of territory. Growth stops or retraction occurs when there are no longer net gains from expansion.

Not all wars may seem to be triggered by careful, rational economic calculations. But even seemingly "irrational" wars may sometimes be seen as having economic objectives.

The costs of maintaining acquired territory have changed over time. Unlike today, in centuries past, ordinary citizens living in some border territories, such as Alsace, were accustomed to the idea that the state controlling them might change; the change of state receiving their taxes would not have drastic impacts on their daily life. When present, this citizen acceptance and obedience to new rulers could reduce the costs of policing newly acquired territories. In contrast, modern takeovers of territory can be challenged by strong citizen resistance, which makes physical acquisition of territory less attractive than previously.

Roman Empire

One of the first stable European empires was run by the Roman state. The economics of financial gain governed much of its creation. The empire was based on expanding out from Rome toward other places, maintaining control and security on transport routes. Rome built faster means of transport than other less organized groups, such as the northerly Germanic tribes. The Romans created a provincial system, in which territory would be conquered, existing political structures largely left in place, and trade would increase. Evidence of increasing trade can in part be derived from Mediterranean shipwrecks increasing substantially from 200 BC to 0 BC. Since taxes could be levied on trade, higher trade resulted in larger tax revenues.

One well-documented example of the empire's expansion is the Roman conquest of Gaul (roughly modern France and Belgium), by Julius Caesar, as described in his History of The Gallic Wars.

In the first few years after the conquest, the Gallic local tribal leaders rebelled almost every year, in some part of the territory as the leaders were not accustomed to accepting external control. They even tried to coordinate their rebellion to create a more difficult challenge for the Roman legions. During the period of initial conquering and tribal rebellions across Gaul, Caesar increased the number of his legions from four to eleven. The increase was necessary to successfully defeat all rebellions and alliances across the Gallic tribes.

For indigenous residents of Gaul, the early years of being a member of the Roman Empire may not have yielded high economic benefits. The residents were subjected to higher taxes (being paid to the empire and its representatives) with few benefits (as trade may not have picked up immediately). In the longer run, economic activity likely grew as roads were built by the Romans and longer trade routes across tribal areas were not taxed by local tribes. Only in the longer run would trade benefits have created improvements for the conquered people.

When the gains from rebellion went down, particularly after a large battle that Caesar won at Alesia, the tribes accepted that the external force of Rome would control their territory. In the meantime, over a small number of years, from 58 to 50 BC, Caesar is believed to have become the richest person in the Roman empire, after initially having to borrow substantially to raise his legions.

The Roman method of territorial expansion internalized economic incentives of the generals and the governing state. One person, the general, would be put in charge of a province or potential province. The general would both pay the costs of the province's military forces and reap gains via taxes and booty from that province. For the territory that Caesar took over, he had to pay the cost of funding his armies, and at the same time he personally received the exclusive right to tax the local population as part of his control.

This linking of military and fiscal powers provided a direct incentive for generals to take over the most productive and economically advanced lands, rather than the ones that were least settled and easiest to take over. The technique also gave the generals an incentive not to demand excessive military support and an incentive to win the long-run support from the conquered people. As a result of the system, generals would only try to take over land when it was directly profitable for them to do so.

The stability of Roman territories encouraged investment in physical assets. As one example of physical infrastructure investment, the Romans built roads that led from their centers of trade and that facilitated defense of their military borders.

These roads are striking engineering achievements. They were constructed by Roman armies in times of peace. These roads were so well built that many remain in use to this day, and the route so well designed that some now lay under European highways. This meant that the taxes paid to armies by conquered peoples were not just viewed as a payment for security and peace. They also generated the preconditions for increased wealth via trade and production. The roads would increase the speed of movement over the Roman territories for carts by a factor of 3-4 over normal dirt roads. This would engender a consequent reduction in the cost of transport, and thus would reduce the price of some goods and increase choice on marketplaces. For example, in France, the Beauce region near Paris was a major grain producing hub but was one month of cart travel from Marseille. After the Romans established a sprawling road network, a cart of grain or flour could travel the same distance in 7 days. This dramatically expanded the ability of people to obtain food and reduced the frequency of local famines.

The Romans also supported better technology for farming. Yields from crops grew to about 10 times the amount of grain that was used as seed; a very high yield from farming for that period. Increased yields may have come from better plant stock, better fertilizing of land and better irrigation where that was possible. With overall output increasing after the Roman takeover, an economic gain was created that could potentially be shared with the conquered tribes, and which could help to defray new taxes. Higher economic activity because of the Roman occupation was manifested in increased trade.

The main cost imposed on the provinces was that for supporting the empire apparatus in Rome and that of the armies. For funding the latter, the Romans had an innovative bonus system. Following the Marian reforms, a professional army was made accessible to those without property, and financed by the generals. Soldiers belonged to a legion with a contract that required 15-25 years of service and work. At the end of that time, a soldier would be given a lump sum value: farmland in conquered territory. Thus, the conquered land would in part be re-allocated to pay soldiers. This mechanism created stable Roman-loyal settlements throughout the empire, with well-trained protectors. This also increasingly moved the cultural and religious foundations of the newly conquered territories to resemble those of the center of the empire. The counter-balancing cost, of this, however, was the constant need for new land.

The lure of riches led many soldiers to show a strong loyalty to the empire. Had they not been soldiers, they would simply have stagnated on the lower rungs of society with no prospect of ever owning land of their own. The military system thus created a system of social mobility that supported the most stable empire in history, one that lasted, arguably, 700 years and ultimately covered an immense breadth of territory.

The determination of borders would be a function of several factors. One key factor would be the economic productive potential of the area. Another would be the defensibility of the border against invaders. In principle, if all land is equally productive in an endless flat geography, a doubling of the area under control results in a border that is less than double in size. This follows directly from the fact that the area of a circle or square, when doubled, results in a less than proportionate increase in the length of its borders. For example, a territory that is 10 miles by 10 miles has 100 square miles and a border of 40 miles to protect. A territory that is 15 miles by 15 miles has more than twice the area (at 225 square miles) but has only a 50 percent increase in border, which rises from 40 to 60 miles. The important point here is that the tax necessary to support an army with a fixed number of soldiers per mile of border, goes down as the size of the territory increases. However, in practice some lands were more valuable than others, such as in the provinces of Africa and Aegyptus. Furthermore, natural defenses such as the Rhine, Danube and Euphrates rivers were used as frontiers for the empire due to their defensive capabilities.

The Romans were repeatedly forced to abandon provinces with lower economic potential and more costly to defend. Despite successfully conquering Scotland in the years 80-84 AD, the Romans decided to fall back and build

Hadrian's wall in the north of England a few decades later. Part of the economic calculation lay in the benefit of preventing external invasion of their territory. As an example of this, just 20 years after building Hadrian's Wall around 120 AD, arguably because of increased incursions by the Scottish, the Romans moved their border wall even further north than Hadrian's Wall, between the Forth and the Clyde, with a new barrier known as the Antonine Wall. This move to a second (earthen) wall is suspected to have occurred for defensive reasons, to prevent attacks from northern Caledonian tribes, rather than out of a desire to conquer and control new territory, and in any case was abandoned 8 years after its construction, presumably because of defensive failures. Similarly the Roman province of Dacia in modern day Romania was abandoned in 271 AD following barbarian incursions. The Romans fell back behind the Danube and heavily fortified it to protect the richer provinces from raids. The movement of boundaries and abandonment of provinces shows that the exact locations of the empire's borders were determined and updated by the relative military costs and gains of each part of the empire.

China

The first Chinese empire, the Qin empire, assembled several large kingdoms, under the ruthless First Emperor of Qin, who died in 210 BC. His empire can be dated from 221-207 BC. It combined previously warring states including the Han, Zhao, Wei, Qi, Yan and Chu states, and included areas that, centuries before, had been Jin and Han as well as Qin. This constitutes an area largely comparable to the China we have today, with the word "China" itself based on the word Qin.

Violence underpinned the economic order that would ultimately create stable production and investment conditions. One battle in 364 BC resulted in the Qin army inflicting 60,000 casualties on the Wei army, creating a massive loss of human capital.

While the Qin emperor's death was followed by rebellions and civil war, within 8 years, in 202 BC, the Han empire was formed, led by its first emperor, Gaozu. He won the civil war through the initial strategy of leaving two-thirds of the territory in the hands of regional kings in exchange for their military support.

At the time there was a debate over which of two possible types of administrative systems was most desirable. The first was a feudal system in which the emperor would allocate his own official territory to local kings and grant them autonomy (Fenfengzhi), and the second was a system of prefectures and counties, with administrative power held centrally by the national government (Junxianzhi). The latter was found to allow the central government to raise far larger tax revenues than the feudal system, without too large of an extra cost, and thereby could strengthen the central government. The Qin dynasty was the first to adopt Junxianzhi. Emperor Han Gaozu, after forming the Han Empire, selected a mix of the two systems, in part because of uncertainty over which system was better and in part because after years of war, the central government was not strong enough to immediately impose Junxianzhi.

His successors, notably Han Wudi, then systematically asserted central power and, within a century, had the entire territory under a unified central administration. While kings were maintained as figureheads, administrators were appointed by the central state run by the emperor. This led to little direct power for the local kings, though they retained a right to benefit from a share of the taxes collected in their historical territories, thus providing them with an economic basis to remain within the kingdom.

In addition to presiding over a wide territory with taxes to support its large standing army, the administration system of the empire was made efficient through a promotion process for administrators based on talent and not noble connections. These created a separate group of gentry who were a scholarly class with substantial power and the essential skills for running a state. These efficiencies, combined with well-focused agricultural techniques leading to high returns on planted seeds, helped to create a stable Han empire, built around a Confucian model of hierarchical respect.

Eventually, the state decided to create a nationalized salt and iron industry. This decision was made during the reign of Han Zhaodi, after a fierce economic debate summarized by Huankuan. The substantial revenues from these industries helped fund the expenses of maintaining armies. They created a new monopoly rent for the central state, transferring it from private hands that had been regulated and taxed by local kings. A more prosperous commercial and agricultural sector, plus the income gain to the central state from salt and steel monopolies, allowed for reduction in taxes as the central state took over the regional kingdoms.

A spirit of compromise created peace and unity during the Han dynasty. With sufficient monetary support from the central government, armies were mainly constituted of criminals and foreigners, creating a separation between the military and the rest of society. Although armies could easily number 400,000 in times of war, this did not create instability. The relatively stable fiscal system helped maintain a steady equilibrium for the society. The Han Dynasty lasted until 220 AD, or about 400 years, and established cultural and geographic frontiers that, though undergoing occasional transitions, have established a stable core that endures more than 2000 years after its foundation.

The adoption of the system of prefectures and counties under central control, along with the nationalization of the salt and iron industries brought the Han Dynasty and the power of its central government to its culmination. This peak illustrates how a strong empire is based upon a sound economic and financial standing. The expansion of empire or governmental power follows a fundamentally economic logic.

The application of this logic continued to affect China throughout its history. In 1793, under the Qing Empire, the Macartney Embassy visited Emperor Qianlong in the hope of building diplomatic and trade relations with the Qing Dynasty. Qianlong rejected all the terms proposed by the Embassy. The reason Qianlong gave was "Our Celestial Empire possesses all things in prolific abundance and lacks no product within its borders. There is therefore no need to import the manufactures of outside barbarians in exchange for our own products." Qianlong saw no economic benefits of opening trade or further territorial expansions. This suggested also that there was no further economic benefit from war.

In economic terms, marginal profit of new territorial expansion over neighbors was considered negative and therefore not worth undertaking. Economic logic thus remained a determining factor over the boundaries of the Qing Empire.

British Empire

The British empire grew fundamentally for economic reasons. It was built via war, diplomacy and manipulation, and rested on its control of the seas and international trade. Control of the seas required superiority in technology, force or skill of war. The defeat of the Spanish Armada was an emblematic moment for the creation of the British empire, leading to a Spanish retreat from constant challenging of the legitimacy of the British state. The core strength of the British navy originated from its technological capacity to project its power with speed and effectiveness.

The British empire was built up largely through administrative skill that facilitated trade. Its institutions promoted trade by private companies with strong commercial incentives to succeed. The importance of commercial agents for creating financial profit is consistent with the notion that an empire can be constituted via commercial enterprise. This point underlies the suggestion that a US "empire" could be supported by the international activities of US-based digital companies.

The British government established monopolies for trade by royal grants to private stock companies that operated in different territories. The East India Company operated in India, and ran the trade between India, Britain and other colonies in the area. Other British trading companies were set up throughout the empire The West India Company (operating trade to the Caribbean), the Hudson Bay Trading Company (covering much of modern Canada), the chartered companies in the North American colonies (such as the Virginia Company of London), the Chinese trading monopolies, and various private African ventures, (such as the Imperial British East Africa Company or the British South Africa Company). All these helped to provide the financial heft for an empire that ultimately extended to cover one quarter of the world's population. Unlike the Spanish and Portuguese focus on the Americas with its gold and silver production, the British empire was centered on international trade of a wide diversity of goods. The British trading companies illustrated an economic model with a close link between military takeover, government activities and private commercial activities organized by shareholding. Great Britain was not unique in using private companies for its empire expansion. In a similar approach, the French colonies also involved commercial ventures, such as the Compagnie française des Indes orientales which was founded by Colbert in 1664 and lasted until 1793. Despite other empires utilizing corporate oversight of colonies, the British ended up with a superior and longer lasting set of corporate relationships, in part because of their superior skills and technology for control of the seas.

In the organization of trade, the British sought to maintain high value-added commercial opportunities for the home country more than for colonies. For example, in the 18th century, the British retained the exclusive right to process cotton, depriving the American colonies of the possibility to profit from this stage of production, and ensuring that significant value added would be kept to the British themselves. At the same time, and as a necessary accompaniment of this, the British maintained the exclusive right to trade cotton, so that the American cotton producing states could not sell outside the British empire.

While Britain designed its empire for its personal benefit, the growth of its colonies during the period of British control may have exceeded that which would have occurred absent the empire. To the extent this is true, the empire could be seen as delivering value throughout the ruled territories from increased trade and productive capacity. This may be one of the reasons it was able to hold together for such a long time, until other sources of supply worldwide reduced the margin available from controlling the internal trade within the empire.

The British Empire remained stable and at a pinnacle for a full century, though ultimately fell apart after World War II. Britain's position of world dominance was lost to its financial dependence on the United States for rebuilding after the war. But it was already weakened by the cost imposed by local resistance in the colonies. The state thus faced the dilemma to invest more in control of overseas colonies or to jettison colonies that had become more expensive to maintain in the empire than to have outside the empire.

Franco-Prussian War: 1870-71

In 1866, German unification began with Prussia's victory over Austria. Southern German states joined and formed the

German Empire in 1870. The German Empire assembled largely around the Kingdom of Prussia after centuries of city states and leagues. The confederation was, in part, in response to the French Napoleonic forces taking control of Prussia after stunning military defeats of Prussian forces at Jena and Auerstädt.

In July 1870, the newly emerging German Empire attacked France. The Prussian and German allied forces defeated the French emperor at Sedan, took Paris and conquered a large swath of northern France. In January 1871, France agreed to a peace treaty that yielded Alsace and Lorraine to Germany, and paid a "war indemnity" to the new German Empire of five billion francs. The nature of this forcible taking of territory illustrates the crucial role of economics in determining the boundaries of empire expansion.

Despite having conquered territory that went hundreds of kilometers further into France than Alsace and Lorraine, the Germans did not seek to keep most of their acquired French territory. Instead, the new German empire retained only the départements of Alsace and Lorraine.

One possible reason for not seeking to maintain control of large, conquered swathes of France is that the German armies would have been too stretched to maintain a tight control over a hostile territory roughly the size of their own country without a substantial increase in the net revenue base. Yet in 1871, governments did not have income tax revenue or revenue such as VAT. Instead, they were financed under a much narrower base of tariffs on trade, taxes on goods entering cities or specific product taxes, like for salt. For example, the city of Paris had tax assessors at its doors, who determined the tax payable on all goods entering the city. Absent a large tax increase to cover the cost of policing France, the aggregate financial gain to Germany from having a broader geographic territory covered that would include Paris would not have been obvious.

In contrast to the rest of France, Alsace and Lorraine were in 1870 more culturally similar to Germany than France, given that their people were mostly ethnically and traditionally Germanic. Alsace and Lorraine had been part of the Holy Roman Empire with princes and city states, before France's expansion into the area for different periods starting around 1552 and extending through gradual expansion under Louis XIII and Louis XIV in the 17th century. The ethnicity of people in Alsace and Lorraine involved Germanic traditions and German language speaking.

As a result of the common ethnicity, a large occupying force would not be necessary. In this situation, the increased tax revenues and economic activity in the rest of Germany generated by Alsace and Lorraine could make the territorial acquisition profitable for the German state. The enormous additional French terrain acquired may have served as bargaining leverage for France to cede Alsace and Lorraine. The Treaty of Frankfurt gave residents of Alsace and Lorraine the right to emigrate to France or remain and become German. The deadline for emigrating was 1 October 1872, giving people sufficient time to sell their homes and move. Only a modest proportion of the population opted for French citizenship (161,000 people) which was about 10 percent of the population. Only 3 percent actually moved, with about 50,000 emigrations. This could indicate that even the residents did not perceive a strong negative economic impact from being absorbed into another empire.

The economic arguments were not exclusively positive for the integration of Alsace and Lorraine with the German empire. While the German Kaiser Wilhelm I opted for integration, there was domestic debate and German opposition to this territorial acquisition within his government. A large part of the debate was economic. In particular, some southern German industrialists were opposed to the increased competition they would have from the Alsatian industrialists, notably the cloth manufacturing business in the Alsatian town of Mulhouse. This opposition arose from the conflict of economic interests that would come about from some businesses losing out as a result of competing expertise in the new territories. The industrialists made a proposal for Alsace to be traded to the other country it bordered, Switzerland, in return for Swiss lands elsewhere. This proposal was not seriously considered by the German government and would not have been likely to be considered by the Swiss. In practice, the national government, through the person of the kaiser, maintained the acquisition of Alsace and Lorraine, suggesting a net economic gain to the German Empire, while the businesspeople most at risk of increased competition opposed the territorial expansion. The German industrialist loss of profits from competition was, from the German Empire's perspective, of less importance than the increased financial strength from the new territories that would accrue to the state.

World War I

World War I can be seen as illustrating another angle of the economic objectives of war, related not to empire expansion but maintenance. This goal of prevention of war was guaranteed by the curious mechanism of commitment to war. That is, World War I originated largely from alliances that were not intended to extend economic territory, but rather to keep territorial balance and prevent aggression.

The origin of World War I is complex. The triggering event was the assassination of the heir of the Austro-Hungarian empire, Archduke Franz Ferdinand by an anarchist, Gavrilo Princip, in Sarajevo on 28 June 1914. This led to a declaration of a war by Austro-Hungary against the small nation of Serbia. At that time, a complex system of alliances existed in which Serbia participated. This was designed to prevent acquisition of one state's territory by another, this "small" declaration of war lit a match that then activated alliances and war preparations resulting in an almost automatic European war. The ensuing two-sided aggression illustrated the danger of overbroad alliances of mutual support. The Triple Alliance was made up of mutual military support agreements by Germany, Austro-Hungary, and Italy, and the competing Triple Entente linked Britain, France and Russia.

The objective of these alliances was to ensure balance that would prevent territorial gains for the Entente or Alliance powers. In short, the alliances had an objective of protecting current assets, an essentially economic purpose. These alliances were seen as one way to prevent loss of territory, as opposed to a positive desire for gain of territory. The expectation was that the alliances would also reduce the likelihood of war by making each side larger in its defensive capacities.

In a tragic irony, the alliances had the contrary effect, though, of leading to a war like no other before and which completely upset the system of balance of power that had been designed to favor the status quo. The war was characterized as the Great War because it involved so many countries, simultaneously coordinating their military actions. In this conflict, the Suez Canal was a key strategic asset for influencing the cost of shipping. The canal allowed merchant, passenger and military ships to come straight from Asia and the Indian Ocean into the Mediterranean, without going through the treacherous Cape around South Africa, considerably reducing shipping costs for those who controlled it and those who were granted access.

Ultimately, even countries that were not in either of these alliances joined the war, as the United States did in 1917. While it had remained neutral at the onset of the war, it joined the Entente after the sinking of the US ocean liner the Lusitania by the Alliance. The Lusitania attack arose from the fact that, even though the United States was officially neutral in the war, it was providing extensive supplies to the Entente powers, and not the Alliance powers, and thus effectively was supporting the war effort of the Triple Entente. This support may have arisen from the economic opportunity to profit from the war and the provision of supplies. Arguably part of this trade preference may have related to the relative security of continuing relationships between traders who were relatively easily accessible via a direct oceanic route, (France and the UK via the Atlantic, Russia via the Pacific) while reaching Germany, Italy and Austro-Hungarian territories from the United States was substantially more at risk of attack, requiring passing through waters under effective control of the Entente. For example, before the sinking of the Lusitania, the British Naval Blockade prevented entry of ships into the entrances of the North Sea and the English Channel, as well as restricting access to the Mediterranean.

The end of World War I had direct economic consequences for the perceived aggressor and loser, with the required large war reparations to be paid by Germany to countries like France, which had experienced economic devastation especially on the frontlines where trenches were dug and bombs rained down. These war reparations were to be paid over a period of many years. As booty for the war, France was rewarded with Alsace and Lorraine and the allies split up much of the Austro-Hungarian empire, such as Transylvania, which was ceded to Romania.

Ironically, while the source of World War I may not have directly been a desire to take financial wealth, the conclusion of the war resulted in the taking of wealth and territory from both Germany and the Austro-Hungarian empire. The taking of territory from losers provides an ongoing incentive to engage in war if one expects to win and if the territory can be sufficiently productive to repay the cost of war and subsequent policing.

The Versailles Treaty that ended World War I is commonly considered to have caused the German economic despair which brought the Nazis to power. It forced the

German state to repay Entente countries 269 billion Reichsmark over 92 years. Inflation rates went so high that it was almost inconceivable to those of us who have lived with stable inflation rates. At its apex of hyperinflation, a loaf of bread that might have cost 160 marks at the conclusion of 1922 would have cost around 200 billion marks by the end of the next year. With the currency in a hyperinflationary spiral, German could not easily sustain international trade, which further increased the difficulty for the Weimar government to make the international payments required by the peace terms.

In short, while the war and aggression were not primarily linked to the desire to gain economic wealth from others, the result was exactly that: the taking of payments from the war's losers. The economic exploitation of the losers by the winners sowed the seeds for the next great war.

World War II

The Second World War was, from the beginning, about territorial expansion. The Germans had developed an impressive and dominating war machine, while pacifists in other countries chose to appease Germany's initial expansions, largely under the view that such expansions were a natural response to the excessive economic demands on Germany coming from World War I. Germany needed to expand to keep its economic motor in full-speed operation and to guarantee provision of key resources that were lacking in its own territory, like oil. The transition of Germany into a wartime economy was made in collaboration with the industrial leaders of the country years in advance of any aggression, further emphasizing the role of economic actors in supporting and profiting from its military buildup.

The Japanese were also interested in territorial acquisition to acquire natural resources. The key oil supplies in the region at that time were in the Philippines. To maintain their new and expanding empire, the Japanese needed guaranteed access to oil supplies. The oil in the Middle East was not reliable, due to the influence over that region by the UK and US. The only realistic military strength that could oppose Japan's expansion into other countries was the US. Its Pacific Fleet with its aircraft carriers gave the United States an impressive capability to project air power almost anywhere in the Pacific. The US colonial position over the Philippines made the supply of oil from the Philippines unreliable from the Japanese perspective. This led to the December 1941 attack on Pearl Harbor in Hawaii, an effort to knock out the US 5th Fleet which, due to preparation for exercises, was all gathered in the same place. The failure of Japan to sink the entire fleet, partly due to bad luck as many of its ships had left the port, was a key error that meant the US remained a major force in the Pacific at the start of the war. After the attack, the US was forced to enter the war against Japan and, by extension, its allies.

In both the first and second world wars, the United States had not initially taken sides in the primarily European battles. Its lack of engagement may have been because of a view that involvement in foreign wars was a waste of US assets. But it may also have arisen from the desire to maintain active trade links with both sides in wartime, as times of war can be economically very advantageous to suppliers who are not themselves engaged in the debilitating process of losing their own people and resources. Moreover, the United States had the particularly complex situation of holding fresh immigrants from the opposing powers. As a result, whatever side the US would take, immigrants from the other side would serve as a domestic opposition to entry to the war. In both world wars, only outside factors, not alliances, drew the United States into war. The sinking of the Lusitania passenger ship by the Germans in World War I was that compelling outside factor, the attack on Pearl Harbor, two years after the Germans attacked Poland, was the precipitating event for World War II.

The end of the Second World War was followed by the loss of major land assets that had been acquired by the Axis powers during the war. However, learning lessons from the First World War, the logic of wartime reparations was completely different after World War II. Those countries that had been decimated did not demand large reparations from Germany. Instead, a general program, funded by the United States and known as the Marshall plan, provided aid to the decimated countries for rebuilding.

The use of force to gain economic assets was not by any means unusual or unique. Rather, war has typically been used for this purpose over history. The United States itself, along with its zone of influence in Latin America was constructed based on these principles.

5. AMERICAN EMPIRE

From sea to shining sea!
> -Katharine Lee Bates, poet, "America the Beautiful"

National Construction

Before discussing the establishment of the 21st century US Internet Empire, let us first look at how the territory was assembled to form the US. The US and its sphere of influence were constructed by the achievement of economic objectives through the repeated application of violent force, or threats of force, including in Latin America. The crucial role of violence and war for this empire is illustrated by the consequence of self-imposed limits on the type and extent of force the US was ready to use in Latin America following the Cuban revolution and the public release in the early 1970s of papers describing the violent and manipulative tools used by the US to influence other countries. This ensuing "principled" era of reduced direct violence coincided with a reduction in US client-state influence, and the decline of the First America Empire.

The initial territorial "empire" was constructed to expand the economic possibilities of the United States. The core territory began with a union of 13 states that ratified the constitution between 1787 and 1788: Connecticut, Delaware, Georgia, Maryland, Massachusetts, New Hampshire, New Jersey, New York, North Carolina, Pennsylvania, Rhode Island, South Carolina and Virginia.

The subsequent expansion to create an empire does not involve territory ruled over by an "emperor." Rather the true nature of an empire is determined by the taking over of substantial territory that is outside the initial boundaries of the country. In this sense, the US expansion bore the hallmarks of an empire. The territorial expansion that emerged from this core was rarely equaled: 90 percent of the current land mass of the United States is an expansion past the initial 13 states.

The construction of the First American Empire consisted of gradual expansion, punctuated with violent military actions. Gains from war, and potential war, were integrally tied not only to the revolution but to the later construction of the entire United States. With a modern perspective, the approaches taken might seem barbarous, brutal and unjust. But such a modern perspective is an artificial construction of modern values on the values of a different time. The important point here is that violence and the threat of violence were crucial for creating the economic and social unit that has become the United States.

While there were earlier expansions, the first major expansion was the 1803 Louisiana purchase, an economic transaction in which Napoleon received 25 million dollars in return for one third of the territory that now constitutes the United States. This sale occurred for two reasons. The first was that Napoleon needed funds for his military ambitions in Europe and the Mediterranean. The timing was in response to the creation of a third coalition in Europe to defeat the French Republic and restore the French monarchy. Thomas Jefferson, who was the US president, but had previously served as ambassador to Paris, sent a delegation to negotiate the purchase of the Port of New Orleans. His envoys, James Monroe and Robert Livingston, found themselves offered the entire territory of Louisiana, encompassing 828,000 square miles of land, for which they negotiated a price of around $2.6 billion in today's dollars. In one of the most remarkable real estate deals of history, the price converted into $314 modern dollars per square mile, or about $100 per square kilometer. This exchange gave the United States the default right to acquire lands by treaty or conquest over indigenous peoples.

The second reason for the sale of the Louisiana Territory was more subtle: the United States had a much stronger ability to exercise military force to take this territory than France had to defend it. As a result, Napoleon recognized that if he did not accept the offer of money, the territory could probably be taken by force. The size of the French colonial population that might have defended it was only about 20,000. These colonists were mostly based in a small part of the Territory, the current US state of Louisiana, and were certainly unable to defend against the broad base of force and settlement that could be applied from north to south by the United States. The US standing army and the natural "zone of economic influence" would easily and naturally lead a movement west from its existing well settled states.

The acquisition of the Louisiana territory doubled the geographic area of the United States. The acquisition was followed by a systematic redistribution and settlement policy to occupy the land by settlers from the east. The policy provided constant opportunities for hardworking and entrepreneurial farmers to obtain land, cultivate it and ultimately contribute to the economic strength of the United States. This land settlement program gave settlers the ability to race to acquire a single parcel of land that amounted to one-quarter of a square mile for each parcel. Land that was not arable would later be distributed in larger lots for private use, like raising cattle. Some of the land from the Louisiana purchase was among the most highly productive arable land in the world. The transition to planted agriculture allowed for more intensive land use and a consequent increase in economic output of the land. Parts of transition, however, were only made possible by the mass killing and deportation of the native American population on both this and later land acquisitions. The subsequent change in land productivity and output, acquired at high human cost, could in principle cover the payment cost of acquisition and expansion into the territory, including the resettlement costs and military costs. More broadly, the United States' frontier mentality, expanding economically intensive use of land into areas with previously low-intensity production, extended from this time, in 1804, forwards through just before the First World War.

Later in the 1840s, the US adopted a concept of Manifest Destiny that suggested an inevitable and natural expansion of the United States to control land through the Pacific. The US government tried on several occasions from 1842 through 1845 to purchase the Mexican part of this land that later became New Mexico, Arizona, California, Nevada, Utah, along with parts of other states including Texas. John Slidell was sent on a mission in 1845 to buy the northern part of Mexico for up to $50 million, but this offer was simply refused by the Mexican government. This territory had, at the time, a low population density, with only about 75,000 Mexican citizens in an area covering one million square miles. It was thus ripe for taking by force, as the costs of overcoming a resistant local population would be low.

Various disputes erupted related to whether the border of Texas extended all the way to the Rio Grande River, as the Republic of Texas claimed, or north of the river by about 150 miles, as the government of Mexico claimed. After Texas joined the United States, as a state, in 1845, the United States decided to invade Mexico. President Polk determined that land then constituting Mexico, running from the border of Texas through to the Pacific Ocean, would serve as a useful addition to US territory for settlement and create the potential for wider coastal trade of its goods, notably to the Pacific. He used a Mexican effort to repulse troops sent between the Rio Grande and Nueces River to instigate a war.

The Mexican American War of 1846 to 1848 was ostensibly justified by a minor incursion of Mexicans at a frontier outpost that was in traditional Mexican territory, the Alamo. The consequence was a follow up military escalation into a large US military expedition, that took advantage of the period of French control, or lack thereof, over Mexico. This opportunistic war involved sending three separate army groups into the territory. General Zachary Taylor's group of 4000 professional soldiers was sent into northern Mexico with the mission to win as much territory as possible. Another group of soldiers, led by Colonel Stephen Kearny, went through New Mexico to California. A third group, under Major General Winfield Scott, made a landing by sea in Veracruz that went into the heart of Mexico in 1847 and ultimately seized Mexico City. A very broad swath of territory was taken through military force. After this conquest, the United States negotiated to return Mexico City and other conquered lands and to purchase the territory it sought between Texas and the Pacific Ocean. This return of territory to Mexico occurred after the US army conquered all in its path over a period of 22 months. Under the Treaty of Guadalupe Hidalgo, Texas through California were purchased for the token payment of 15 million dollars. The Mexicans accepted the offer due to absence of any effective alternative and the limited Mexican population that could justify fighting to keep the land, as well as the offer of peace over core territory to Mexican nationality. There was potential on the newly acquired land for much more intense usage, with a consequent possibility of economic gain. It also presented strategic importance for the United States for ports and passage of goods between Asia and North America, a strategic importance that was missing for Mexico, which already straddled the Pacific and the Atlantic, via the Gulf of Mexico. The Mexican land also had some potential for planted agriculture given the presence of the Rio Grande River which was ultimately used as a source of water for widescale irrigation many decades later.

Around the same time, in response to good fertility and empty lands in the "Oregon Country," which included Washington, Oregon, Montana, Americans began moving to the area and quickly very much outnumbered the British Hudson Bay fur traders working in the beaver pelt trade. In 1846, to avoid war, the British government agreed on a line that would divide Canada from the United States at the 42nd parallel, keeping Vancouver Island as part of Canada.

The US actions followed from the principal that military Strength would be used to obtain and expand economic strength. The construction of the core First American Empire was therefore completed before the First World War, with the two subsequent states to be added, Alaska and Hawaii, already under the control of the US. Alaska was bought from Russia in 1867 in part due to the difficulty for Russia to protect it from possible British invasion; Hawaii was already under formal US influence since 1898 when it became a US territory partly under the influence of US business magnates who wanted control of the islands to lie with the US government.

First American Empire: Projection of Influence

Once the US had obtained its west coast with deep water ports in San Diego and Los Angeles in the south, San Francisco in the center and Seattle in the north, the US economic interests further led to its interventions overseas in ways that protected property and market exchange systems. This projection of US influence was particularly strong in Latin America.

Even before the US Mexican war of 1846 to 1848, the US asserted its unique right to intervene in Latin America, with the claim under the "Monroe Doctrine" of 1823 that foreign powers should not intervene in Latin America. This assertion was, at the time, not taking account of the influence of Spain and Britain in the area. Nonetheless, over time, Latin America fell much more strongly in the zone of US influence than of any other country. Control over Latin America was expressed via a principal that any intervention there by foreign power would result in war and through the subtle, or non-subtle, manipulation of regimes to deliver pro-American governments over the years.

The extension of US power and interests was by no means limited to Latin America. During the Cold War, it regularly intervened elsewhere where it had a strategic economic interest to do so. The battle to prevent socialist revolutions around the world can be seen through the lens of retaining zones of like-minded trading partners. If a country aligned with the USSR, that move would be followed by a loss of trade and of any US-owned economic assets in the country. This economic rationale underlies much of the geopolitical positioning of the cold war that raged between the end of World War II and the fall of the Iron Curtain around 1990.

The US Empire expansion over the continental United States and Alaska was stable, in contrast to these instances of failure to hold an expanded zone of influence. One reason is that the indigenous population was smaller than the population of settlers, due to the much larger capacity of settlers to generate economic value from a higher food output and thus greater population per square mile. This use of settlers to outweigh the local population is a classic strategy of empire building aimed at stabilizing control.

This strategy was not used for the empire's expansion into Latin America. Instead, the expansion was supported by a client-state model that meant territory remained foreign with control by local politicians using local forces and only occasional direct use of force by the US.

Such an approach prevents the costs of resentment that arise from direct foreign control. But the protection of the client-state from external interference cannot prevent popular rebellions. These were driven by repressive policies of US-supported dictators, and the desire for redistribution by the less advantaged who, in a true democratic state, would constitute the majority. Another reason for the loss was low investment of US government resources into the client states, as the economic gains through indirect control were limited and insufficient to justify high expenditure.

Up through the 1970s, low-cost forms of political intervention were apparently sometimes used by US intelligence. The CIA even had an assassination program known as Family Jewels. This could be viewed as an extension of use of force for economic gain.

Political assassinations were no longer permitted starting with President Gerald Ford's Executive Order 11905 that forbade US government employees from conspiring in "political" assassination. This was promulgated following investigations by the Church and Pike Committees of the Senate and House in 1975. For the US political leaders, there was a direct danger to them, once such programs were known, of tit for tat behavior by forces from other countries who, suspecting an assassination, might retort with revenge assassinations against US politicians. Fidel Castro, for example, is reported to have said to the Associated Press in Havana in September 1963 that he understood the Americans were trying to kill him and that, if that continued, retribution would follow.

As a result of the banning of political assassination by

Executive Order, the difficulty and cost of maintaining the preferred leaders around the world substantially increased as their political opposition could not be eliminated. Ultimately, client-state obedience became harder to guarantee, as Latin American countries from Brazil to Mexico had increasingly real democracies, with outside oversight of vote counting and with limited ability to give bribes to leaders. It is no coincidence that with the cessation of assassination programs and the increased focus of the US on ethical statesmanship, including via elections, the grip of the United States on its Latin American "backyard" substantially lessened.

Latin America subsequently experienced substantial political movements to the left and a loss of economic benefits of US allegiance. The absence of popular support for the US, and the hostility against client politicians raised the potential for rebellion, resulting in higher costs of maintaining the order and stability necessary for commercial success of the empire. Since the ratio of costs to benefits of maintaining the empire increased, the economic gain from the client-state empire in Latin America would increasingly fail to exceed the costs of the security and administrative apparatus. Specific experiences in Cuba, Nicaragua, Venezuela and Brazil illustrate the loss of US influence in Latin America.

Cuba

In 1898, after the US warship USS Maine mysteriously blew up in the Port of Havana killing three-quarters of its crew, at a time when Cuba was a Spanish colony and the US was supporting rebels against the Spanish power, the US declared war against Spain. Over a ten-week period of hostilities in the Caribbean and Pacific Ocean, Spanish naval forces were defeated in the battles of Santiago de Cuba and of Manila Bay. The US forces obtained the surrender of Havana and Manila. The Spanish-American war concluded with Spain ceding its colonies to the US, and Spain receiving modest compensation for infrastructure investment it lost in the Philippines. The effective support and control of Pro-American regimes in the Philippines continued in this country even after the loss of power of Ferdinand Marcos.

The importance of maintaining the influence acquired in external territories was considered essential as a bulwark against the risk of a wave of socialist revolutions that would have expropriated US investments and changed the balance of world trade and power. The revolution in Cuba was the most embarrassing reversal of this century-long policy. The Russians suddenly had potential bases close to the United States, which until then had the monopoly of bases close to other foreign territories, but no hostile bases close to itself. This existence of USSR influence in the US backyard of Cuba was a shocking change in geopolitical stability and was treated by the US as unacceptable. Having enemy powers in the backyard of a major empire is destabilizing and may create more of a geopolitical problem than an economic one.

The revolution in Cuba that resulted in the Castro forces taking power in 1958 must not be misinterpreted: it was a popularly supported revolt against a largely corrupt regime that received support from American corporations and the US government. The initial main opponents of the revolution were US banana producing companies, that owned enormous plantations, as well as US controlled casinos and hotels in seaside resorts, a mere 82 miles from the US border. Subsequent immigration, largely to Florida by emigrants who escaped Castro, created an internal political force within the United States that has often sought hostile relations with Cuba.

The revolution led by Fidel Castro culminated with his taking power from President Batista in January 1959. This regime ultimately became anti-American, as it lacked funds and quickly found a route to government finance by expropriating US property. The young Castro government defeated the 17 April 1961 effort at counter-revolution, the Bay of Pigs landing by Cuban exiles who were both financed and directed by the CIA. Under the ongoing threat from the US, Cuba became increasingly close to the USSR, a proximity that culminated on 14 October 1962 with a US spy plane photograph showing the assembling of an SS-4 medium range ballistic missile in Cuba. Under Kennedy, the US government threatened war with the USSR over the placement of the USSR missile bases in an island only 90 miles from the US border, missiles that would have been impossible for the US to intercept before they reached US soil. This standoff finished on 28 October when the USSR withdrew its plans for missile bases in Cuba in return for withdrawal of US nuclear missiles from Turkey.

Nicaragua

The experience in Cuba could not be viewed as the falling of the first domino in Latin America. Cuba was not the only nor the original Latin American country to select a leadership that was contrary to US interests. Nicaragua provides a useful illustration of US efforts to maintain influence in Latin America. In 1909, the US President Taft commanded the overthrow of the Nicaraguan president Santos Zelaya. In 1912, the US intervened with 2,300 marines to protect American property and influence, and install a pro-US government. Through 1933, it kept a marine detachment there. The Nicaraguan government of the time consented to this presence. After an election in 1924, the marines left the country.

However, soon afterwards, further US troop support was requested. In 1927, an uprising by peasants against the US occupation and the Nicaraguan establishment was started. This ended when the national guard, under Anastasio Somoza Garcia, captured and killed the leader of the uprising in 1937. The Somoza family then governed Nicaragua until

1979, when the Sandinista uprising became a successful revolution and its leaders came to power.

When Nicaragua flipped to an anti-American government in 1979, the US began providing support under Carter to the historic dictatorship of the Somoza faction. This continued under Reagan, though the executive branch support of the Somoza regime was dealt a blow when the US Congress forbade further funding to the anti-Sandinista Contras. This was the point at which the White House set in place a secret plan to provide weapons to the Contras, via the exchange of arms for drugs. The US could argue that the arrival of the Sandinistas to power had itself been supported by foreign powers. Moreover, the Sandinistas were alleged to provide supplies and encourage revolution in El Salvador, which General Ortega from Nicaragua allegedly admitted in 1985 and 1986.

The US involvement in Nicaragua led to a 1986 case before the International Court of Justice, which the US refused to recognize. This case, brought by the Republic of Nicaragua against the US, resulted in a judgement from the Court that the United States was "in breach of its obligations under customary international law not to use force against another State" but was not found guilty of direct human rights abuses, though it was found to have encouraged them through a manual on psychological operations in guerilla warfare. In 1985, the US withdrew its agreement to the Court's Compulsory Jurisdiction. The United States refused to recognize the International Court of Justice's jurisdiction and blocked its enforcement at the level of the UN Security Council. These events with Nicaragua illustrate how the US was ready to use the force of war to support its economic interests and had a history of doing so.

Venezuela

From the US perspective, the rise to power of the left-wing populist Fifth Republic Movement in Venezuela in 1999 is illustrative of the problematic outcomes of revolution. One election created a regime change that resulted in expropriation of US company property while the control of the election apparatus prevented changes away from the controlling regime.

Under the US's new approach to diplomacy and war, the post-Monroe doctrine, the United States did not intervene with large military force in Venezuela, despite losing US business interests in the aftermath of Chávez's victory in 1999. The citizens of Venezuela could argue that, through their revolution, they were retaking the benefits of their oil production, and thus receiving direct economic gain.

The Bolivarian revolution resulted in a self-determination facilitated by the presence of oil. However, the economic management has been weak, leading to an ongoing economic crisis, with GDP contracting by 25 percent in 2019 alone, according to IMF estimates, and inflation having reached 4,000 percent in 2017. Since the revolution, about 90 percent of international companies that had been based in Venezuela are estimated to have left. Oil production has fallen dramatically from about 3,453 thousand barrels per day in December 1997, before the revolution, to 392 thousand per day in July 2020. This decline arose from lack of equipment, technology, personnel and knowledge. Between 1999 and 2022, substantial US economic trade with Venezuela has been lost as a result of the change in political leadership.

Brazil

While political movements may move away from the US camp in Latin America, the pendulum may sometimes rock back towards popular support for more market-oriented policies, once citizens realize the extent to which any government can be corrupt or incompetent for creating a stable state and good job opportunities.

This type of popular swing of the pendulum is illustrated by the 2018 vote in Brazil that installed a more rightist regime under Jair Bolsonaro after a series of scandals and prosecutions involving politicians and bid rigging and bribes on a variety of contracts, from the building Olympic stadiums in Rio to the allocation of service contracts for oil extraction. President Lula, from the center-left Worker's Party, along with his chosen successor Roussef, were all tainted by scandals. Roussef's impeachment in 2016 and Lula's corruption conviction in 2017 may have been illustrations of more subtle US techniques for influencing political outcomes. One confidential email that was leaked and allegedly written by Lula's prosecutor Deltan Dallagnol described his prison sentence as "a gift from the CIA."

Under President Bolsonaro, Brazilian hostility to the US reduced. The government considered allocating oil exploration contracts, allegedly of interest to US companies, rather than running the exploration itself via the state-owned oil company Petrobras. The change in government illustrated how economic benefits could come to the United States and its businesses from the change in leadership of Brazil.

Overall, the first economic empire has been of tremendous benefit to the United States. It created a coast to coast, fully controlled structure of recognized US territory, with substantial natural resources, agricultural capacity and geographic unity. It also granted access to other countries' markets and resources for US companies. This first economic empire, though, had limits when it projected outside the direct acquisition of new territory that would be bolted onto the US.

Because the United States did not take ongoing military control of Latin American countries but rather sought to install friendly regimes, the ongoing costs of maintaining the external empire have been limited. But the gains have been limited as well, as one of the greatest government gains from controlling a territory or an economy come from the direct taxation of its companies, citizens and resource extraction.

The US government restraint may have arisen in part from Latin American citizens' known hostility to the US interests as well as low aggregate GDP figures in these countries. This hostility would make exerting permanent direct control costly in terms of policing, while the low GDP would make the gains from control low. The approach of the US has thus been to advocate and influence outcomes in external relations and only occasionally use military interventions, otherwise preferring lower cost interventions. As a result, the gains from ensuring the survival of market systems aligned to US trade accrued only diffusely to local business and their leaders. This approach left enormous potential benefits of empire building on the table, untouched by the US in those countries even where there were ongoing client-state relationships. The areas with relatively weak US influence included most of Europe, Asia and Africa.

It is these untouched possibilities for benefit that make possible a Second American Empire operated over the Internet.

Second American Empire

The Second American Empire is the digital empire. It is not based on control by physical territorial expansion because such expansion is no longer necessary for economic control. The "empire" is based on international expansion of virtual control by US-based internet companies. In transactions with these companies, the commercial contractor is, in essence, in the US. When dealing with foreign customers, the corporate control over the transaction is American. It is in this sense that the empire exists, with "virtual" transactions around the world under the control of American companies.

The decline of US influence in Latin America did not

imply that business no longer mattered to the US. Rather, the pragmatic approach to foreign relations, built on linking business interests with foreign influence, has been a cornerstone of the US economic success. Prosperous business interests was crucial for obtaining good trading relations and stable property ownership elsewhere, even after its change in treatment of client-states. The loss in prominence in Latin America arose from reduced willingness to use violence. But this reduced willingness is a precursor to increased focus on non-violent expansion of economic activity.

From an economic perspective, this Internet Empire is a continuation in the line of previous empires and territorial expansion by war. The astonishing and rapid success of this fundamentally economic empire arose because the First American Empire left a lot of potential gains on the table. It also arose because US enterprises, and the US financial system, have so far been superior in innovation, marketing, and expansion possibilities to those of other countries.

One could thus imagine a second thesis, proclaiming a New Manifest Destiny: the United States corporate sector will dominate the world internet business enterprise because of its better management, better agility, better financing structure and better innovative capacity. The US government in turn has fully engaged to further its corporate interests through direct, aggressive and successful research policy and diplomacy, thus laying the groundwork for a fully operational Internet Empire.

Other countries with comparable corporate advantages could also potentially achieve Internet empires. China already has world leading internet companies and has many of the same underlying innovative, management and financing features as in the US. It could be next. But China has not yet massively projected its internet strength in Europe, though TikTok has become a broad user success. Further Chinese success could well arise in the future, if not held back by western government restrictions on Chinese digital products. The US projection of internet strength seized the opportunity with its historic allies in Europe and benefitted from an early corporate focus on multi-lingual product availability.

This Second US Empire, the New Manifest Destiny, is precisely the subject of this book. The United States have, piece by piece, often through pure luck and chance, but also from knowing how to recognize and profit from such chance, constructed a new digital empire. Its reach extends across the world, via fiber optic cable and satellite. Its subtle model involves the creation and takeover of selected commercial activity by US companies. This takeover is backed up by well executed US government policies domestically. It is also backed by the government's international policies that have supported open trade in the digital sphere. While this takeover does not represent all or even most of the economic value added, the full extent of affected economic activity remains difficult to quantify under current economic accounting standards. A lower bound of the valuation of internet corporate enterprises, of roughly 10 percent of global stock market value, may not be sufficient, as it ignores the other value added in "non-internet" companies that are nonetheless trading over the Internet.

The logic of internet expansion into foreign territory has been one of economic interests, just as with prior wars and physical expansion of territory. When the profits of adding a new territory exceed the costs, efforts have been made by the US companies to expand into new territory. The benefits are the additional profits that come from a new territory. The costs are the marketing and extra human resource needs that come from the expansion. The economic value of the expansions has been, in many ways, the sort of value that would merit traditional wars. But the beauty of the Internet Empire has been that the costs did not include military incursion, and the methods did not require violence or ongoing policing. Instead, the expansion has occurred through natural means of customer adoption of US platforms and US solutions, thus reducing one of the main costs of prior exercises in territorial expansion.

What is clear is that over the last 100 years, economic activity has shifted away from agricultural dominance to service sector dominance.

As the share of agriculture control has declined, the geographic/economic importance of land has become less based on agricultural capacity and more tied to natural resources for extraction, such as petroleum, iron, copper, uranium, lithium, potash and diamonds. Land without such resources now accounts for only a small share of the value chain. This leaves the value of economic activity largely independent of agriculture. The value is in services or natural resources.

The access points for sale and advertising of many goods are increasingly provided over the Internet, with even local services such as food and haircuts being provided via an internet order. This is the new frontier. As consumers flock to platforms for ordering and reserving their services, platforms derive direct value from control over transactions without any need for physical control of land. The modern empire is thus decentralized, does not require expansion with armies and does not need to show any open hostility. Moreover, much of the new takeover has delivered real extra value, deep business model innovation and fundamentally given customers what they want. This takeover should therefore not be viewed by customers as a takeover by the enemy. Non-US governments increasingly recognize the results of a war have been gained on the backs of loss of control of economic activity within their borders and the decline of local industries. But they have not known how to react to such a peaceful expansion of economic influence.

Evolution of methods of expanding the zone of economic control

Wars have typically been fought to extend the physical territory of the aggressors or, when acquisition was not the initial origin, as in World War I, the result of the war was acquisition of territories by the victor. This approach to fighting wars, which can be viewed as going back to the earliest times of tribal conflict, was largely based on the principle that land and people provided the greatest economic asset. While controlling territory did not necessarily give the right to profit from the territory directly, it provided the capacity to finance armies, to protect borders and the capacity to tax transactions, or production, in such a way that the victor would gain from the taking of territory. Empires would remove border-based taxes that increased the cost of internal trading, build better infrastructure and enforce better rules for business. These changes would yield a stronger environment for investment, innovation and a reward to hard work. As a result of extra value created, successful economic empires could support armies that would resist foreign incursions and maintain local domination. After these costs, surplus would still provide comfortable lives for their ruling class and for innovators and investors.

In a modern age, land does still have value, especially when natural resources are on it, such as oil, gold, diamonds, or when it is prime agricultural territory. But the main value now lies *outside* of agricultural land, with agricultural activity having diminished to less than three percent of GDP in most OECD countries. The primary value in expanding a country's territory comes from the ability to tax transactions made by individuals and companies. Government taxation has risen to levels that account for 40 percent or more of economic activity, primarily through the combinations of sales or VAT taxes, income taxes, capital gains taxes, and corporate taxes. Tariffs, which used to constitute a major tax base of governments, have now been much reduced.

The rise of services and the reduction in tariffs have jointly created an opportunity for a new kind of empire, built around the Internet. Will it last? Examining the decline of other empires throughout history can help answer this question, by focusing on the economic fundamentals that might favor long survival or a short period of predominance.

6. THE NATURE AND FALL OF EMPIRES

There is an enormous difference between starting a company and running one. Thinking up great ideas, which requires mainly intelligence and knowledge, is much easier than building an organization, which also requires measures of tenacity, discipline and understanding.
-Robert X. Cringely

As a result of corporate successes without one centrally led decision structure, the United States has, in aggregate, established an Internet Empire. We define an "empire" as an entity with a large or predominating size in geography and commerce. The commerce is here not restricted to direct activity of the country's government but can apply also to private entities expanding the economic reach of the country. As examples of key private sector roles, the British and French Empires were constructed, in large part, with commercial enterprises. The concept of empire can include the US internet companies, with their enormous net of activity that proceeds all the way to dealing directly with foreign customers. We are not limiting the discussion to the largest US internet companies of Alphabet, Amazon, Apple, Meta and Microsoft. Rather, many more digital companies than those in the top 5 in the US are also active in the international expansion. The Second American Empire's broad spectrum of internet and technology companies have reached a stage of growth in which they have increasingly taken over productive economic activity outside of the national borders.

To understand the implications of this empire, it is worth looking at why empires have prospered and failed. Some empires have lasted hundreds of years. This is the case for the Roman Empire and a number of others. In the end, many of these have ultimately lost sway. We will see that the typical reasons that empires fail do not apply to the US internet empire. In fact, in the case of the US internet expansion, we may expect a stable empire, which is all the more remarkable as a result of its decentralized management structure. Thousands of different companies and major investors have independently taken decisions that have created, expanded, and consolidated the US business success. There is no king to determine the steps that are to be taken in managing the empire. There may be some exceptional venture capitalists, like John Doerr or Peter Thiel, who have served as a common element to multiple successful business enterprises, but this factor should not be over-emphasized because exceptional businesspeople exist in all cultures.

This success may be due in part to the system of physically concentrated human capital that developed around Silicon Valley. But it can also be attributed in large part to a host of factors that might arise in greater amounts in the US than elsewhere, some of these being relatively little studied, others well documented. These include:

1. The incorporation of business needs into the legal system;
2. The US system of property rights;

3. A psychological desire to win inculcated by American schools into children at a young age;
4. The combination of top-level technical and business training;
5. The military industrial complex;
6. The tax structure;
7. A lenient bankruptcy structure; and
8. The frontier mentality inherited from the US's early history.

Many of these features of US society are often critiqued. For example, within media and political science discourse in the US, the lobbying power of business to influence domestic rules is a frequent topic, and is typically viewed negatively. Yet the US growth rate is consistently higher than European countries with lesser corporate influence. Perhaps the high business ability to lobby makes up for a democratic deficit arising from the fact that large businesses have no direct voting power.

In a market economy, business creates most economic success. One can reasonably hypothesize that an economy is more likely to facilitate business success when business itself has a more direct route to influencing power. A society with no business power would include an election system controlled by the median voter. Despite many advantages of such a system, it will often have the effect of punishing business. The reason is that from a self-interested perspective, median voters may be most interested to lower their own taxes and raise taxes on business and on those with more income and wealth than them. The balancing between these two needs, of business on the one hand and society on the other, is based in large part on legal systems and societal values. This balancing affects the extent of business power. A country with a large capacity for businesses to influence the business environment in ways that favor productivity and business expansion is more likely to raise successful businesses. This may be precisely what has happened in the US. The overall US legal and governance system is designed around allowing and enhancing business success because this ensures the productive capacity is present. This productive capacity is in turn a powerful creator of jobs.

However, recognizing the close US linkage between business and government, the question must be posed of whether the US digital dominance is permanent or fleeting. The answer depends on the underlying economic conditions of the expansion. As long as the economic conditions favorable to this digital empire remain, it is likely that the digital strength of the US will survive.

To see why this digital empire might nonetheless fail, it is worth examining why some empires have not survived the test of time. For the moment, the features of the digital expansion seem to avoid the historical pitfalls that have led to decline of empires.

Why Empires Fail

When wars over territory have been successfully won, the primary reason for not consolidating long-term control is lack of support among the local population.

The presence of physical force on the ground was an essential ingredient to maintaining peace, and hence ensuring that an empire's expansion could be economically profitable. The takeover of third-party territory can be driven by many reasons, such as economic expansion, the attraction of controlling natural resources, the possibility of looting, and the possibility of religious expansion. But active opposition to the new power can require expensive policing which is in turn costly.

Fall of Rome

After many centuries of maintaining its empire, the

western Roman Empire disintegrated. The reasons for this are complex, but one likely contributor is that the empire no longer had the financial power to fund its armies and government apparatus. One reason for the decline of Rome's military financing capacity was that its territory was not growing sufficiently to pay its soldiers with land. The Roman system of providing retired soldiers with farmland would not work well without conquering new land. For many centuries, the Romans had regularly gone to war to capture new territory. However, when they reached a size in which the new territory would not be productive for arable farming, or in which taking the land from indigenous inhabitants would create too much opposition, farms could no longer be used for compensation for years of loyal soldiering service.

Another reason for decline is that disease ravaged the empire on several occasions, reducing its tax revenues. For example, the Antonine plague of 165 to 180 AD decimated the population and raised the cost of agricultural labor. Evidence from Egyptian documents suggests substantial loss of tax revenues at the same time. In another example, the Plague of Cyprian, that lasted from 249 to 262 AD, also decimated the population. There is evidence of decreasing trade activity from reduced presence of shipwrecks in the Mediterranean following these two events. Two centuries later, around 450 AD, Rome may have been ravaged by malaria, with the first known evidence of malaria found in a village in Lugnano near Rome.

While a plague would decimate the empire's population, and thus tax base, the length of frontiers to guard would not change. Plagues would thus change the ratio of revenue to costs, putting a heavy strain on the Empire's ability to maintain its dominance over its extended holdings.

Partly in response to different strains across the empire, in 395 AD the Roman Empire was divided into two parts, the Western and the Eastern Roman empires. The western empire was more subject to attacks because of its extensive borders with central Europe. Rome was sacked by the goths in 410 and 455 AD.

The decline may have come from the financial difficulty of supplying a large and inherently unproductive army of several hundreds of thousands of soldiers. In an epoch when 80 to 90 percent of the population was working in fields, the large standing army placed a particularly high burden on the Roman economy. Ultimately an army of sufficient size to maintain the empire could not be supported.

Genghis Khan and the Mongols

The harsh weather and difficult living conditions in Mongolia created an ideal environment for raising formidable warriors. Considering both the Mongol's skill at winning battles and limited resources at home, the Mongols went to war to seek the economic benefit of improved living standards by annexing or plundering new territory in the grand pursuit of creating an empire spanning from east to west. But they did not create sufficiently stable economic governance mechanisms to establish an empire that would last.

The military prowess of the Mongol soldiers came from their training as fast-attacking horsemen who were skilled archers from the saddle. Their cavalry had unique capacities to attack and retreat quickly. While retreating, they could shoot arrows at their enemy, and at the opportune moment would turn around and charge against the disorganized pursuers. They are claimed to have copied many of the strategies of wolf packs, known for their agility, astuteness and cohesion. Their destructive cavalry fighting methods could break all but the best trained army.

In 1206 the Mongolian chief Temüjin achieved the unification of the Mongolian tribe and was acknowledged as Genghis Khan (universal leader). He then led the Mongol efforts to extend Mongolian control from 1205-1209 into the

Chinese kingdom of Xi Xia. This feat was followed by the broader conquest of northern China, at that time ruled by the Jin dynasty. His army then moved on to extend its conquests as far West as Turkey and modern-day eastern Europe.

Success required a focus on the economics of running an empire, ensuring that internal economic conditions were better than without the empire, deriving sufficient stable revenue from increased output to cover the administrative costs of the empire and the profits necessary for business investment. The empire needed to ensure that the flow of payments to the government would support a united leadership rather than breaking up into smaller parts.

Unfortunately for their empire's longevity, the Mongols military prowess was not matched by organizational strength and discipline. As one example, their army conquered Hungary, but abandoned this acquisition for its leader to return to run in the election of a new "grand khan." After resolution of its leadership challenge, the Mongol army then took different territory, in Iran and Syria, having abandoned that in Hungary.

They did seek to take over key aspects of existing kingdoms, making sure that the territory could pay for its apparatus and was well run. Taking over an existing empire would, in principle, seem a technique for ensuring their success. But they also had policies that often destroyed economic value where they took over, notably by establishing a credible pattern of territorial expansion. Before an attack, they would offer an opportunity for peaceful annexation. If that offer was rejected, the following attack resulted in wholesale slaughter, enslavement and sparing only of people with special skills.

During the reign of Kublai Khan, fifth Great Khan and grandson of Genghis Khan, in the late 13th century, the empire increasingly divided its management, with him expressing the strongest interest in controlling China and moving his capital to Beijing. In doing so, he neglected his overlordship of other dominions of the empire like Syria, where his control lost its strength. In 1279 he took over the Song kingdom of southern China and treated its rulers well, preventing a great slaughter than would have followed under prior Mongol practice. This strategy paid off because southern China had the world's most prosperous economy at that time. His Yuan Dynasty ruled China until 1368.

The extent of taxes under Mongol rule created particular resentment among peasants, along with rules that forbade them from killing animals that were eating their grain. Most importantly, if synergies for the whole were not created by having the parts together, the empire would not be stable. Taxes must yield positive benefits for those paying them, otherwise taxpayer resentment fuels incentives for rebellion and overthrow of rulers.

Ultimately, the Mongol empire did not last. The Mongol experience illustrates how having a strong army and successful war leaders was not sufficient to build an empire. Their motivations for military aggression were often based on plunder, which is inherently short run, and the desire to take control of trade routes rather than a long-run economics-focused strategy of stable territorial control.

While the Mongol empire survived in various permutations for more than a hundred years, its dissolution ultimately arose from lack of economic synergies between the different parts, in addition to weak rulers and lack of control over differing political factions among the Mongols.

Colonial control of China

Much later in China, during the period of forced opening by Britain, increasing quantities of tea for Britain were bought and paid for with cotton and opium from India. The Chinese authorities sought to restrict the trade of opium, which led to a war started by the British in 1840 resulting in their control of a trading zone in Shanghai. With Nanking under their cannons, the Treaty of Nanking was signed in 1842 that assured a number of ports would be open to British traders, that criminal charges against British citizens would be handled by British courts and that tariffs and duties would be limited in size. Other colonial powers moved in with similar demands, thus preventing Britain from having exclusive trade rights with China. Trade with China was facilitated by organized opium imports that literally addicted Chinese consumers to foreign trade products.

After less than a century of colonial control of trade by Britain, France, Germany and the Portuguese, the Boxer Rebellion of 1900 occurred. This movement was organized by peasants against both the Qing and the West. The rebellion advocated for a resurgence of the Ming. The poorly armed and disorganized peasant rebellion was crushed by a coalition of colonial powers.

This rebellion was followed by the more modern and profound 1911 (or Xinhai) revolution which was a society-wide rebellion against imperial rule and in favor of a rule led by the people and with a scientific mindset.

By the end of the 19th century, the imperial system was politically and economically outdated. The 1900 rebellion and the 1911 revolt made the cost of maintaining foreign armed forces high. The costs of a military force that could control the country likely began to outweigh the profits from trade. This change in the economics of the colonial control meant that the foreign armies could neither guarantee peace nor secure the Chinese imperial leadership.

With the profits from trade insufficient to cover the military needs, the balance of colonial influence waned. The subsequent loss of support from the local Chinese empire leadership led to the expulsion of the foreign forces and traders in the late 1920s.

The declines of these three empires illustrate the crucial need for an enduring empire both to be accepted by the occupied population and to ensure that the economic profits from the conquest continually outweigh the costs of maintaining control and security. These criteria for long-run success are likely met by the new Internet Empire.

7. WHY THE INTERNET EMPIRE IS BETTER THAN AN OLD-STYLE EMPIRE

They wonder much to hear that gold, which in itself is so useless a thing, should be everywhere so much esteemed, that even men for whom it was made, and by whom it has its value, should yet be thought of less value than it is.
-Sir Thomas More

The core thesis of this book is that the modern-day internet structure is economically equivalent to what, in prior times, would have been an empire acquired through aggression into new territories. In the past, the core benefit of economic empires was driven by the economic value of land and market power over trade. But these sources of value have now changed.

The value of land-based activities has shrunk

Increasingly, land has been relegated to a secondary role in most countries' productive capabilities. From the initial beginnings of human civilization, land was at the core of economic value and employment. The reduction of the rural population over the last 100 years is emblematic of the declining value of agricultural land in economic activity. This is not an old phenomenon but a transformation that is still underway.

As an example, consider the village from which my French wife's family originates, a small village called Darazac in Corrèze. It shrank from a population of about 630 between 1793 and 1891, to 537 people in 1921 during a period with relatively modest technological advances for agriculture. With the dramatic technological changes since then, the population has now fallen to 138 as of the 2016 census of the population, with more than 50 percent of these residents being retired.

This is demonstrative of the percent of the labor force working in agriculture in France as a whole, which has fallen substantially over time. In 1400, the farm share of labor in France was estimated to be 71.4 percent. This fell to 61.1 percent in 1750, 59.2 percent in 1800 and 8.4 percent in 1980.

In the United States, according to economist Stanley Lebergott, the share of US farm labor force of overall labor was 72 percent in 1800, 54.8 percent in 1850, 40.2 percent in 1900, 12 percent in 1950 and by 2015, this figure had fallen to less than 2 percent.

The UK experienced a much earlier industrialization of its workforce than other countries, with its share of the male labor force in agriculture at 44 percent in 1755, falling to 35 percent by 1813-1820, 14 percent by 1920 and 1.5 percent today. The UK's early industrialization was achieved thanks to innovations, such as the steam engine, to the presence of easily extracted natural resources, and to an excess of population over what was required for servicing its land's agricultural needs. The empire also benefited greatly from having the value added of the transformation of raw materials, such as the processing of cotton, in the UK rather than in the colonies.

These examples are not exceptions. They exemplify how the historical dominance of agricultural activity over other areas of activity has fallen in developed economies, though at different rates and different times. (See Figure 1.) Consider how agriculture has ceased to be the core economic activity of economic life: whether measured by the value of economic activity, or the number of people working to produce food, the share has fallen in most countries, from more than 50 percent to less than 10 percent, and often less than 5 percent. The economist Thomas Piketty shows how this decline in activity is associated with a relative decline in the value of agricultural land in the total capital stock of countries. These declines in agricultural employment share and simple land value suggest that a modern war to obtain agricultural capacity could yield lower economic gains than in the past.

Figure 1. Share of labor force employed in agriculture, 1400-2019

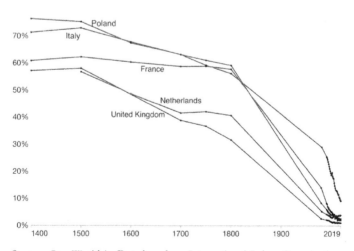

Source: Our World in Data based on International Labor Organization (via the World Bank) and historical sources (in references)

Exceptions to the decline in farm-based labor include former communist countries like Poland, which still had 29.1 percent of the labor force in agriculture, as of 1981, and Italy, which still had 14 percent of the population in agriculture as of 1980, or Romania which had 43 percent of its labor force in agriculture even as of 2001 and 23 percent as of 2016. These countries had lower salaries for non-farm labor and lesser degrees of industrialization and service economy activities than others. The declining share of agriculture in overall economic activity is nonetheless common even to these countries.

A large part of the change in employment in agriculture comes from higher productivity on farmland. For example, cereal yields in the UK rose by a factor of 2-3 times between the 1950s and 1990s, while the US experienced a nearly five-fold increase in corn yields per acre after 1940. Chile experienced a much later increase in yields, but that did nonetheless happen, with 2-3 times increase in cereal yields between 1980 and 2015.

In addition to farm products, the other primary products of fishing and mining have constituted a small share of economic activity over the last centuries. For example, in the US, fishing and mining accounted for only 0.8 percent of employment in 1800 compared to 73.7 percent for farming. In 1900, the added share of fishing and mining to farm employment was 2.4 percent, still indicating a modest employment value of fishing and mining compared to farm-based production at 40.2 percent.

Mining and natural resources may still constitute large shares of economic value in some countries and regions. This applies both to legal and illegal outputs. For example, in the Middle East, oil and gas (and their derivatives) still constitute a high share of output. In Saudi Arabia, for example, the share of oil and gas in its GDP has typically lain around 40 percent and gone up to 77 percent in 1979 when oil prices were at a peak.

In Angola, oil accounts for around 50 percent of GDP. The oil and gas shares of GDP for oil producing countries vary substantially with the world price of crude oil. In Botswana, Zimbabwe and Angola, diamonds still constitute a high share of output. Angola alone is estimated to have produced 3 million carats of diamonds in 2003 and possibly 10 million by 2007.

Illegal drug production can also be an important and high-value agriculture product in some countries. In Colombia and Afghanistan, drug production is considerable. Colombia allegedly accounted for about 43 percent of worldwide coca production in 2009, for an unknown share of Colombia's GDP. Afghanistan accounted for about 90 percent of the world's opium crop, and more than half of the country's legal GDP, despite the post-9/11 occupation of the country by US-allied forces.

In these countries with high value resources, such as oil, diamonds and drugs, instability and likelihood of civil war is higher than elsewhere. Examples of this are the years of FARC activity in Colombia, Taliban activity in Afghanistan, and civil war in Angola and Sudan. One reason for this instability is that the production of natural resources is easily transferred from one "owner" to another, so the gain from fighting to control the territory with these resources is very high, much higher (per acre) than from taking over pure agricultural land and much easier to manage for a new regime than the takeover of industrial production facilities. In many countries without stable governments, a resource curse has developed, with egregious abuses committed in the name of obtaining and profiting from resources.

Making matters worse for such countries, business strategy precepts suggest that industrial production locations should be focused where possible in countries with political stability. Countries with a higher likelihood of civil war are thus less likely to have large industrial production capital (like factories) that can be expropriated by a new regime after acquiring territory.

As a result of the decline in share of agriculture, the value of acquisition of agricultural land by force is much reduced. The value of land with natural resources, however, remains high and therefore can be an economic rationale for aggression and discord over control of rents.

The value of service and non-agricultural goods has come to dominate economic activity

Service sector activity has come to dominate many developed economies. Modern economies of developed countries are more based on people and less based on land or large capital investment. This change has profound implications for the value of taking over territory of a such an economy. In effect, the country that takes over new territory cannot rely on relatively simple processes to exploit natural resources or capital. It must instead provide a full economic incentive system for promoting service production.

Services have become large shares of economies whether one looks at the allocation of labor to goods (industrial and non-industrial) or services. Services have also become large when one examines value added.

For example, in the United States, as of 2018, services represented 80 percent of labor force occupations, industry 19 percent, and agriculture 1 percent. The finance industry alone has risen to take up 7.5 percent of GDP by 2010 from 2.5 percent in 1947. In France by 2017, services accounted for 79 percent of GDP, with its industrial sector accounting for 19.5 percent and its primary sector 1.7 percent. In the UK, as of 2018, services accounted for about 80 percent of GDP. Of this, about 8.6 percent of GDP comes from financial services, with legal activities amounting to a further 1.4 percent of GDP.

Similar findings apply to other countries, with particularly strong de-industrialization across the most developed economies.

The ability of aggressors to take over the productive capabilities of conquered territories has been made difficult by the rise of the tertiary sector as a share of the economy. In particular, some of the highest value forms of service, such as finance, have many products that are easily moved across borders. The difficulty of taking over services may be one reason for lower rates of war post World War II than were historically found in Europe over the period from 1600 to 1950.

Much of the delivery of the value of these service and goods activities is potentially linked to the Internet

The Internet is the ultimate disembodied service product.

Digital economic activity can be produced from anywhere, and is therefore a potential tool for gaining economic activity in other countries, without having a substantial, or even any, presence in the country.

The complexity of cross border interactions for internet products can leave one dizzy. For example, an internet search for an English pub near the Tower of London can be typed into a Dell computer in Malaysia, using the search engine in a browser, with the query processed by a computer database whose master copy is kept in California while to speed up the answers, the question is actually run on a duplicate database operated in Singapore. The answer could be sent back to the user in Malaysia with the information about pubs close to the Tower of London and the possibility to reserve a table at one of them. The information can also include ads that are targeted at the Malaysia-based user, considering all the information that the search engine knows about that user. These ads could be paid for by companies from around the world, potentially pubs near the Tower of London,

TripAdvisor in the US or pubs in Malaysia. Stating in what jurisdiction the advertising transaction occurred is a challenge that illustrates why internet businesses are hard for governments to oversee and tax.

While most services can be delivered from across the world some regions have determined that they want specific services, such as cloud storage, to be offered exclusively within the control of their jurisdiction. The European Union has insisted on such a solution. One reason for installing this geographic boundary on the Internet is the concern that information stored in other jurisdictions can be easily accessed from foreign, and potentially hostile, authorities. Corporate secrets, confidential government information and personal information could be accessed by order of a legitimate foreign authority, like the US security court, if the storage is based in the US, or Chinese authorities if the storage is based in China. Edward Snowden leaks suggest that information could be intercepted on the way to these services before it reaches the servers of the private companies storing the information.

Geographic boundaries have their limits. The right to be forgotten rules that allow a European resident to erase comments they made on an internet platform is limited geographically. Only European-based users will not be able to access the deleted content. Foreign users, such as American ones, may still access it. The US companies and courts have determined that the right to be forgotten would not be global on the grounds that once information is available in another jurisdiction, it is public in that other jurisdiction, and no one should have the right to erase public information. Providing for a broad right to erase public information could be used to control history and eliminate true facts and opinions.

The former importance of physical geography has been replaced by the internet's geographic enhancement from location capture by devices such as mobile phones.

Physical products are inherently based around the place in which they are offered. For example, a potato bag in a store of North Boston is offered to customers whether they come to the store by foot from down the street or drive down from Vermont.

The Internet has changed this and allowed for creation of products that take into account where a user is. Many businesses now show different information to a user depending on where the user is located. Ride-hailing services like Uber, for example, can customize their offers depending on customers' location. This feature of the Internet thus does build in a geographic component, but that of the user rather than that of the provider.

Maps for driving services may show advertising to users based on where they are, and could, for example, suggest a Burger King coming up in a mile based on the route the person is following. Thus, advertising can be customer specific. Moreover, the impact of advertising can be directly observed. Google can monitor whether a cosmetics store that advertises to a person in a shopping center, over a Google product, actually visits the store. If the phone includes payment features, they may even be able to tell whether a product was purchased and how much was spent by the customer on products on that shopping visit. It is because of this type of geographic monitoring that Google can tell what the busier hours are for stores. This is a potential benefit for consumers who want to lower their time of waiting in queues. But the geographic customization also could allow a malicious watcher to observe who one is meeting simply by knowing the geographic coordinates of two or more users.

Search platforms are increasingly set up with an economic model that helps them to harvest customer value

The ability of internet companies to harvest customer

value involves a set of core economic features that distinguish some of these businesses from more traditional brick-and-mortar businesses. These features include network effects, "single-homing" by users, the ability to scale up in size without comparable increases in physical or human assets, customized pricing and market power on one side of a market. While these effects may also exist in non-internet goods, they have emerged at a new scale with the internet age.

Some services may have very few viable alternatives for a typical user, such as Google search or Facebook. In contrast, some other services and products, such as those involving internet-based ordering and delivery, may still include large degrees of competition with traditional forms of in-store purchase.

Network effects exist when the addition of extra users provides value to existing users. When a new user is added to a messaging app this can be beneficial not only to the new user but also to existing users who have access to an expanded set of contacts. Network effects can help to solidify market power, if it exists, by making it difficult for a service to be replicated by a competitor and can help to sustain market power, once created.

Many internet businesses can add new consumers without a substantial increase in costs. For an internet company to add a new user may require a slight increase in bandwidth capacity of the business, but would not require development of new software, as the existing software can easily be rolled out to new users. This means that internet businesses can scale without "mass," that is without having to make substantial new investments for extra consumers. These businesses can be said to incur low extra costs of serving an additional consumer, though they may have made substantial investments to create the underlying software that is then scaled.

Much of the activity of the internet companies,

particularly for advertising, relies on harvesting wide-ranging information about individual consumers. For example, an internet company may know where you are, what your interests are, what stores you have been to, how much exercise you undertake, the characteristics of your friends, and many other individual features that can allow them to predict your behavior and interests. This can help to customize advertising as well as prices to individuals. More generally, pricing can be customized to the user. Airlines might customize prices to be higher on searchers who are using an Apple computer or for mobile phone users than desktop users. One reason for such price customization could be that externally observable features like phone quality can be associated with greater willingness to pay.

Platforms often use their information on customer preferences for the purpose of matching the customers using the platform with the sellers. Overall, the two-sided features of a platform can be used to create a group of users on one side of a market, such as restaurant delivery users, who the platform essentially helps to advise on where to buy food. This means that restaurants will be willing to share more of their customer value with a platform that has relatively loyal, or single-homing, users who could not have been accessed easily by the restaurant without using the platform. The ability of a platform to serve as a gatekeeper to users gives it market power over sellers who wish to reach those users. This market power has the potential to be used to extract greater value from users and could ultimately raise prices. Products for which market power has been alleged by competition authorities include search and advertising, app stores and exclusive arrangements or contracts that prevent suppliers on a platform from selling elsewhere at a cheaper price.

These harms can be very substantial. Market power can result in increased prices for everyone, as well as higher prices after price discrimination to particular users. The greater market power reduces the share of consumer surplus and business surplus, and reorients those surpluses to platform owners. Competitive forces may no longer work for some platforms that have lock-in and switching costs for platform users, or in which there is a zero price offered on one side of the market that distorts normal market incentives.

The dominant internet economy benefits like an old-time Empire from its worldwide internet dominance, and the consequent harvesting of customer value around the world

The US is benefitting from its broad control of the Internet with larger tax receipts for its government, lower unemployment, increased incomes and higher shareholder returns that are harvested mainly by American investors. This benefit is indirect, in the sense that it does not come from government ownership of physical assets nor from government control of law enforcement systems worldwide. But the financial benefits to the US from the control managed by its companies is incontestable.

From a tax perspective, the US has been a particularly strong beneficiary of this activity, consistent with the theory that a government has an incentive to expand its influence to foreign territories only if the benefit to itself of doing so outweighs its costs. Detailed data on how much tax is paid country by country is not released by the digital companies (just as it is not released by most multinationals). This absence of information makes clear discussions of tax differences more difficult. The impact for digital companies is particularly challenging, due to uncertainties over where value is created and how much should be attributed to intellectual property and design that may be developed in different jurisdictions from those of primary operation of a company.

In contrast, in terms of tax receipts from internet companies, countries besides the US and China have had minimal gains and probably substantial losses. A report by Fair Tax Marks in the UK suggests that overall, the top digital companies have greatly underpaid tax in non-US countries, in comparison to normal tax rates. The report states that over the period of 2010 to 2019, "the gap between the expected headline rates of tax and the cash taxes actually paid was $155.3 billion." The bulk of this gap would come from the lack of tax payment outside the United States, due to two thirds of booked profits coming from foreign activity and a lower taxation rate being applied to foreign earnings. Overall, foreign tax charges amount to about 8.4 percent of overseas earnings by the companies, and any US taxes on foreign earnings top out at 10.5 percent, a particularly low percentage compared to the US level on domestic earnings of 21 percent.

Google, for example, has stated that "Like other multinational companies, we pay the vast majority – more than 80 percent – of our corporate taxes in our home country." At the same time, they note their support of increasing tax clarity and development of new tax principles at an international level. In 2019 Google stated that its global tax rate over the prior 10 years had been over 23 percent, in line with the 23.7 percent average statutory rate across members countries of the OECD. Nonetheless, the Fair Tax Marks report suggests that "cash tax" paid was only 15.8 percent, with the tax rate on foreign profits being even lower, with just $1.25 billion booked on its $19.1 billion profits in 2018, leaving a booked current tax rate of only 6.5 percent.

Facebook paid £28.6 million in tax in the UK in 2018, while recording £1.6 billion in gross revenue from advertisers. Further, Fair Tax Marks suggests that, according to some observers these advertising revenue figures are underestimates, and that revenues "actually raised in the UK" may be double that amount, or about £3.4 billion.

In turn Apple argues that "Under the current international tax system, profits are taxed based on where the value is created. The taxes Apple pays to countries around the world are based on that principle. The vast majority of the value in our products is indisputably created in the United States – where we do our design, development, engineering work and much more – so the majority of our taxes are owed to the US." The implications of this approach at a foreign country level are dramatic.

Some information on foreign taxes paid and, to some extent, revenues, is available for the UK due to its reporting system of data for registered companies.

According to filings of Apple with the UK's Companies House, its two UK subsidiaries had revenues of £1.472 billion in 2020 while paying UK taxes of only £9 million.

In contrast to these UK figures, it is worth noting that Apple has paid worldwide corporate tax of $14.5 billion in 2021, a 50 percent increase from the previous year and a level that would be equivalent, if paid to the US, of about 7 percent of total US corporate income tax payments coming from a single digital company.

In Europe, Apple, which was sued by the European Commission for favorable tax deals received in Ireland, has won an initial appeal against the European Commission's decision on the grounds that the company did not receive a selective benefit giving it a competitive advantage. The suggestion of the court is that the benefit could be received by other companies as well. But the combination of corporate rules in Ireland, the Bahamas and The Netherlands may have allowed large amounts of what outsiders might consider earnings to go untaxed and even stateless in some cases.

The companies named in these studies and cases would likely assert that they are simply following the law and doing the most they can to support their shareholders, as they are indeed obliged to do under their fiduciary duties. This is a fair point and suggests the problem is not on their side but on the side of the international tax system.

Indeed, governments have sought to implement a new system of corporate taxation, with a controversial global minimum corporate tax rate of 15 percent agreed by 136 countries in 2021. The effectiveness of the deal remains to be tested, and is unlikely to resolve the unequal distribution of digital earning profits, as it does not affect the destination of tax receipts. That is, even with a minimum tax rate, the place of taxation of the earnings would be the US for US-based companies because that is where the production is deemed to occur for digital services, not the place where the users are. Efforts to negotiate a new tax deal for digital profits, to replace a Digital Service Tax, are underway. Austria, France, Italy, Spain, the United Kingdom and the US have announced in October 2021 a plan to roll back digital service taxes and retaliatory US tariff threats when a new agreement is finalized on where profits are taxed for digital companies. But the US quite reasonably protects its self-interest and sees little reason to enter an agreement that is not beneficial to itself. Deadlines for progress are continually pushed back, with the OECD Secretary General suggesting in May 2022 that no implementation should be expected before 2024.

Additional questions that are rarely asked, but should be, are about high US benefits from the *personal* income taxation of digital workers and investors, along with pricing advantages of the digital goods and services relative to foreign countries.

Personal income taxation is a greater source of tax revenue than corporate taxation. If we look at US government revenues of $3.42 trillion in 2020, personal income taxation accounts for a whopping $1.6 trillion while corporate income taxes accounted for only $212 billion, or under 10 percent. Personal income tax yielded 7.5 times the amount from corporate income taxation. On top of income taxes, payroll taxes could be considered as coming out of personal earnings, accounting for another 36 percent of government revenues.

Looking at earnings statistics for 2020 in the metropolitan area of San Jose, which includes the headquarters of 3 of the top internet companies, computer information system managers have an average income of $235,040 and software developers have an average income of $157,480. These technical jobs yield earnings of 3-5 times and more the national average earnings of $56,310. These higher earnings convert more than proportionally to higher levels of personal income tax, because the US has a progressive system of taxation, like most OECD countries. The effective rate of taxation would be 32 percent in the range of $164k to $209k compared to income tax rates of 17 percent for an average earner, meaning that good internet jobs will contribute almost four times as much income tax as a typical employee. While it is difficult to estimate the precise income tax gain to the US of hosting the headquarters of big internet companies, the gains are certainly substantial, and potentially of a comparable scale to that of corporate income tax.

Unlike corporate income taxes, these personal income taxes are not a matter for international tax disputes. Nonetheless, they are a substantial additional economic gain to the US from having its Internet Empire. Note that this tax gain to the US government from US workers applies, to a large extent, whether the workers are themselves foreign-born or not.

Another tax gain to the US government arises from capital gains taxes. Most of the owners and founders of the main companies are US residents. To the extent that the large US internet companies are US-investor owned and that their investors pay US capital gains taxes upon realization of the gain, the potential return to the US government from this tax is nontrivial. Consider that the long-term capital gain tax benefit of roughly 15 percent to 20 percent could amount to $600 billion on the created value of the five largest US internet companies. This capital gain effect could, at its maximum, amount to three or more times the total US government take from corporate income tax, which, for reference, is about $200 billion per year. These personal income and capital gains taxes are accruing only to the US but based largely on activity that occurred outside the US.

In terms of consumer pricing advantages, it appears that prices in the US for digital goods and services are lower, on average, than in non-US countries. The Fair Tax Marks report on digital tax suggests, provocatively, that "58.9% of total profits and 50.6% of total revenues are identified as being foreign over a decade." Taken at face value, this would imply that the overall margin on products sold by digital companies outside the United States is about 17 percent higher than in the US. If correct, the precise reasons why prices for digital goods and services may be lower in the United States may relate to a variety of factors, like different types of demand and competitive conditions. Nonetheless, for many years, if not decades, non-US Apple customers from many countries have found purchasing products cheaper in the US than in Europe.

This is not to suggest that other countries do not benefit from the spreading of US internet companies. Most obviously, citizens in foreign countries benefit from the services these companies provide, such as search results, entertainment, communication and mobile services like ridehailing. Moreover, internet companies have been careful, to some extent, to spread out good jobs, with research centers established in other places besides the United States, such as the UK (with Microsoft), France (with Facebook and Google), China (Google, Microsoft) and Ghana (Google). Jobs in these centers go beyond operational tasks, taking advantage of local expertise. Platforms provided by digital businesses provide tremendous opportunities for local business to sell their goods and services both domestically and internationally.

The costs to the internet companies of this territorial expansion are consistently lower than the revenue surplus that is achieved from the expansion

One of the key points we have learned about territorial expansion via classic war and occupation techniques is that the cost of war and occupation must be more than covered by the other profit gains to an empire from the expansion.

In state-expansions of territory, in which governments obtain the property rights to a territory that was not initially under their control by violent means, the property rights may deliver some higher value than internet expansion, because the state would be able to tax all economic activity, rather than solely digital production. On the other hand, the war-mongering state must pay substantial costs for the takeover and occupation of territory. If small numbers of dissenters can increasingly create higher costs, the cost-benefit calculus of war-mongering territorial expansion may not be in favor of territorial expansion. Empires have frequently failed because these costs of occupation were simply too high and unsustainable.

In contrast, when the expansion occurs via private enterprise, the certainty of this profit from territorial expansion is undoubted. This is because we can be confident that profit-seeking companies would not expand further if the costs of expansion outweigh the benefits. One can expect that private, profit-oriented calculations of such gains will be more reliable than that of an empire where decisions are not always made from the perspective of balance sheets and income statements.

The power of the internet business model arises from the fact that its expansion allows for "scale without mass" with relatively low extra costs from expanding outside the initial territory, and with the base costs not depending on the location of users. This means that many internet businesses can easily grow their platform, once created, without necessarily undertaking a fundamental reinvestment in their initial product each time they expand to a new country. The telephone, as an infrastructure-based service, took about 75 years from its invention to reach 100 million customers. Facebook brilliantly managed to achieve this same feat in less than 5 years. The game Candy Crush Saga is the ultimate champion, though; it achieved the 100 million user mark in only 15 months.

This expansion is low cost and can occur due to the underlying economics of internet businesses, with a pre-condition of cheap data processing and cheap data movement. Data processing costs have fallen over the last decades at an exponential rate; the so-called Moore's Law, invented by one of the founders of Intel, suggesting that computing power would double every 18 months or so. At the same time, the increased share of households linked to the fiber optic cable network has allowed for a dramatic reduction in the cost of moving massive quantities of data across geographic borders.

This argument is not intended to suggest that there are no particular costs of international expansion for digital businesses. But these pale in comparison to those of maintaining an occupation force after a traditional type of invasion.

The costs of expansion include those of opening local offices, costs of lobbying, costs of trying to influence public opinion and, increasingly, fines from governments that have found certain of the behaviors of such companies illegal. While the corporate spending on lobbying is relatively low in Europe compared to the US, the cost of defending against various regulatory investigations is increasingly high. During 2022, The Netherlands competition authority fined Apple €5 million per week starting in January 2022 for failing to implement a decision about how it should operate its Appstore for dating websites. This fine occurred because the regulator found fault that Apple's requirement that payments of 30 percent be made for certain app products over its Appstore. Apple responded by charging a 27 percent fee on "sales" instead. The Netherlands competition authority found that Apple violated the competition authority decision multiple times until the weekly fines ceased.

The costs to digital companies of falling afoul of regulator decisions are likely to rise substantially in the future. They may need to rise to a level that gives the companies a financial incentive to follow the law. Under the Digital Markets Act regulation for Europe, companies found in violation of the rules will be subject to fines that can rise to 10 percent of their global annual turnover. For the most egregious violations, companies may be excluded from the EU market according to the final draft of EU legislation. In addition, private lawsuits by injured users are increasingly pursued both in the US and internationally. Private lawsuits have been filed against the Apple, Google (Alphabet) and Facebook (Meta) around the world.

In the future, companies will increasingly have to bear the cost of customization of their content, software and hardware to different geographies. This customization cost may be a relatively small share of their revenues, when one takes into account the fact that large internet companies change their software and experiment on a regular basis.

On the content side, one can imagine that internet companies will have to somehow ensure that their content is not used to foment illegal conspiracies, as Parler is accused of doing during the storming of Capitol Hill in January 2021. Their content will also need to convey true and accurate impressions. In March 2022, a lawsuit was filed by the Australian competition and consumer protection authority, the ACCC, against Meta for not doing enough to stop advertisements for crypto investments on Facebook that implied endorsement from famous Australians, without those endorsements having been given.

On the contractual side, digital services must comply with different standards across countries. While in many places, hotels are not able to charge public prices below the retail price on Booking.com or Expedia, the rules vary. By a special 2015 law, hotels in France, are permitted to charge lower public prices than online travel agencies.

On the software side, companies may be required to invest in modest changes to their programming for different jurisdictions. For example, California has a law that requires companies to make disenrolling from their digital products as easy as a single click on a disenroll button. As a result, cancelling a New York Times subscription in California is easy while elsewhere figuring out how to cancel a subscription can be complicated.

More generally, companies may be required to change their cancellation policies by jurisdiction. Casual experience suggests that some smaller internet companies that charge clients hundreds of dollars a year sometimes have cancellation experience for their enrolled clients that is unduly complex and possibly designed to be non-operational. In one example for which I have the documentation, a company requires that cancellation be done by phone, within a short time window of dates from the annual contract renewal. In some cases, cancellation requests must be dealt with by a specific department that is supposed to call the client back to finalize the cancellation. However, this department may often fail to call the client back.

One might ask: is it not fraud to take people's money when they have not agreed to it, or no longer agree to it? The answer is that, contingent on the contractual details, it might be construed by some courts as fraud. Governments have been asleep at the wheel for not bringing claims against internet companies that enroll and maintain users without their full agreement, and for not writing suitable laws or setting in place enforcement to protect consumers.

Government action in this regard is particularly important to the extent that smaller companies, without a broad reputational risk, do not have an individual incentive to make cancellations easy. In contrast, companies with a high-integrity management or large reputational risk are likely to design cancellation processes that work better for users.

The impacts of the digital expansion and Second American Empire are distinct from those of classic war, largely because of their private features.

Some of the effects of the digital expansion of predominantly US-based companies are comparable, on at least a modest scale, to the results of territorial takeover by war. In many respects, this digital expansionism may be more beneficial for the US than a physical takeover of territory. Taking over territory by force and against the will of a population is often unprofitable, absent large natural resource endowments or broader strategic defensive concerns. Taking over digital territory has many fewer costs. Two subtle contrasts are particularly notable: the role of the population and the role of property rights.

In terms of the population, people both people in and outside the US have been fundamentally involved in the spread of US internet businesses. US companies' expansion is the product of their aggregated individual decisions. The reasons for their decisions to use US internet businesses are, in very large part, that these businesses offer desired product features and that they are particularly good at customizing their products to evolving customer demands. Google, for example, managed to achieve a higher penetration of its browser and search share in Europe than in the US. This follows, in part, from excellent business decisions in its early days, such as to focus on European language and translation in its products. In contrast, in Korea, Google was slow to the gate on language and Naver and Daum dominated the market until recently.

As for property rights, new property rights and contractual relations have been acquired as a result of private digital company expansion. These rights are not US government owned, as they would be after a takeover of territory by classic war. These property rights are not inalienable, as they can ultimately be constrained and limited by regulations. Moreover, recent experience has shown that, in the presence of extremely hostile relations, the use of certain services, like Facebook or Instagram, can be taken away from users, as occurred on 5 March 2022 in Russia. Taking away such a right is nonetheless a technical challenge, because even while Russian servers can block Facebook.com connections made directly, it is difficult for them to block virtual private network (VPN) connections to Facebook.com as these do not proceed directly from a user to the site. In the aftermath of Russia giving its citizens a 2-day notice that access to services like Facebook was going to be cut off, the usage of VPN services in Russia reportedly increased by more than 2,000 percent.

Remarkably, when TikTok, a Chinese-owned product became successful with US users, the US President demanded that, unless it was sold to western interests, its access to users would be cut off. This was a remarkable intervention by the US government in external ownership of internet assets popular with American citizens. This intervention is fully consistent with the hypothesis of creation of a US-dominated Internet Empire being supported by the US government. The demands by Donald Trump almost resulted in the sale of the US operations of TikTok. While the sale did not occur in the end, the non-sale may be attributed to a change in negotiating position under a new president after the 2020 election.

The US expansion of territorial economic control via private companies, ironically, has not been accompanied by equivalent threats to those that the US used against TikTok.

The advantage of privately led expansion as opposed to direct government action is that the economic power benefits from broad acceptance by citizens in the expanded territories. The US digital companies have expanded with the active cooperation and acquiescence of the people in foreign territories. Such expansion has an even more important consequence, private companies are better able to sense, evaluate and appropriate commercial opportunities than most slow-moving governments. When a government uses companies as its emissaries, the companies can assess and act quickly and decisively. Moreover, the digital domain allows for instantaneous spreading of new products, as well as experimentation with new products. For example, Facebook gave its engineers permission to perform experiments of product variations that reached under 10,000 users. This helped to maintain the culture of moving fast that was emphasized by the company's top leadership.

Why the Internet Empire is potentially stable

The new Internet Empire of the United States, which has largely been constructed with no central organizing force, but rather thanks to excellent management and good supporting efforts by the US government, contrasts in many respects with prior efforts of empire building. Most obviously, there is no need to exert physical control over local populations. Consumers make payments electronically, in most cases, and then the profits are repatriated across borders due to absence of capital controls. Moreover, independent citizen decisions have led them to use the services that they deemed best suited to their needs, to which they made commitments before these services were making substantial profits. Thus, internet companies conquered economic activity in both the US and elsewhere product by product, under pure market forces. The internet companies that have gained support from local populations are excellent products that attract the loyalty of local populations, as with Facebook. In Myanmar, the population is seemingly not aware of the Internet as a whole but is much more aware of Facebook.

Even when people leave one platform, they move to another. The ones they move to are typically operating from within the same country, the United States, so the profits from these users go to the same country and, ironically, sometimes even the same company. For example, the Apple ecosystem includes Apple TV and Apple Music, in addition to deriving revenue from Appstore sales of products that perform similar functions.

To prevent market power from being augmented by acquisition, the US Federal Trade Commission started a lawsuit in December 2020 against Facebook to unwind its previously completed acquisitions of Instagram and WhatsApp.

One obvious but notable feature of the Internet is that while transactions appear local to the user, being on their computer, the management can occur thousands of miles away, with local distribution of physical products being the only sustained area of expansion onto local territories.

Internet companies often take advantage of addictive user behaviors to increase consumer retention on their platform. Creating addictive internet services resembles the use of imported opium by the British to create dependency among users in China during the 19th century. Video platforms such as Tik Tok with their continued improvements to its video recommendation algorithms, and with their use of default playing of subsequently selected videos, is absorbing to many users. This pattern of dependent behavior encouraged by the algorithms reduces our ability to concentrate and will potentially have devastating social and productive consequences if these skills are not recovered.

This modern-day opium can be seen on the metros and buses in big and small cities around the world. It can be seen in the way that videos are watched everywhere, and the way that people seem happy with the takeover of their lives. It can be seen in reduced time spent reading. It can be seen in the way that children's natural habits of exercise and play are disrupted, with consequent increase in behavioral problems and obesity.

Think about the claim that the Internet is an addictive substance. Addictive behavior is present when people have an ongoing desire for a feeling, they seek it out in an uncontrolled way, and it delivers a mental release of endorphins. Some types of addictive behavior, such as running, may be beneficial to humans individually and to society more generally, by keeping a fit population and reducing society-wide costs of medical care. Other types of products are increasingly recognized as addictive, such as sugar, an observation that is unlikely to surprise anyone with young children. Well established companies have long realized the effect of sugar, even putting sweet sugar tastes into pacifiers for babies. Yet sugar-using companies are (probably fortunately) not regulated in the same way as cigarette companies.

Considering the definition of addiction, we can all ask ourselves the uncomfortable question, "Am I addicted to the Internet?"

The truth is that most of us probably satisfy the definition of internet addiction. The urge to consult messages, a social network, news, videos, or games leaves many people checking their phones every hour, or even more often. This is not a controlled behavior, but one that has become sub-conscious and deeply ingrained. During work hours, it may be appropriate to look at work messages. But the acceptable sides of addictive behavior may be exceeded. People increasingly look at phones during meals, during meetings, when in bed with a partner, as the tendency has moved to people being online and connected 24 hours a day. Some companies, such as German car manufacturer Volkswagen, have restricted the ability to send and receive corporate emails to working hours only. France has even introduced in 2017 a "right to disconnect." Companies with more than 50 employees must determine the hours when staff are not supposed to send or answer emails.

These steps towards living in a parallel digital world have happened naturally, step by step. The behaviors individually may seem normal. But in aggregate they are not. The opium of the Internet has made many consumers accepting of the dominance of internet companies over their lives. But when we are faced with an addictive product, it is, at the minimum, our individual responsibility to control our use of it. In a 2003 poll of the American Academy of Matrimonial Lawyers, which had responses from 350 divorce attorneys, two thirds reported that the Internet played a significant role in divorces. Given the large social costs of divorce or mental health problems, one may wonder whether the state should play a larger role. Government could set up incentive mechanisms that ensure companies allow sufficient controls to parents, reduce mental harm and prevent excessive time being spent on the Internet.

In the case of children, digital addictions may have particularly bad consequences, ranging from not only life-risking obesity and mental health problems, but also reduced ability to focus, reduced time on learning/homework and increased likelihood of suicide. According to the whistleblower Frances Haugen's revelations in 2021, Facebook research showed that 13.5 percent of teen girls felt that Instagram makes thoughts of suicide worse, and 17 percent felt that it makes eating disorders worse. Such impacts may be relatively small in some instances, but relatively large in others. Their existence shows that commonly used products are not immune to risk. Yet the community engaged with these products keeps coming back.

Internet companies are not taking always responsibility, even though they are at least in part accountable for these negative impacts. At the minimum, they should be more closely overseen. In the long run, one may legitimately ask whether the parties responsible should be made to pay the social costs of increasing mental health and behavioral problems that result from the systems they set up. Otherwise, user addiction only yields benefits to the companies. The addictions keep users coming back in a repeated and stable way, helping to establish the durability of internet dominance.

The United States government has taken a systematic set of positions internationally to ensure that this strong commercial position can be achieved and, to some extent, to limit ability of other countries to prevent this dominance.

(A)   Stopping or reducing discussion of dominance in international forums such as the G20, G7, OECD, UN

The United States government recognized early that the potential for digital businesses was strong and has acted consistently to aid national firms. US government efforts to limit discussions of market power have been significant. For example, in a variety of international forums in which the US is a member, ranging from the G20 to G7 to OECD and UN, it has sought to change wording of documents to either not mention their digital companies, or to change wording related to their activities. For example, efforts to use the phrase "winner take all markets" were consistently changed from initial drafts of international organization documents to either not mention digital companies or, if the members insisted on such mentions, changing the phrasing to "winner takes most markets." This phrasing can be seen in ministerial declarations from OECD, G20 and G7 meetings going back to 2017.

(B) Stopping international efforts at regulation of data and internet companies

Efforts by other countries to start discussing international regulation of internet companies coordinated by an international organization were sought by many countries but always derailed by the United States government, often with the support of other Anglo-Saxon countries like Australia and the UK.

(C) Controlling the core domains

The United States trailed its feet in giving any international oversight to the Internet. The transition from outright military control to international control started on a slow path when internet governance was transferred from the Defense Advanced Research Projects Agency to the United States' National Science Foundation (NSF) at the end of the 1970s. As commercial usage increased, the NSF entered an exclusive contract with the US company Network Solutions, Inc. to sell registry domain names in the dotcom space. Until 1996, the NSF organized the expansion of internet architecture to include international domains, like .cn, .de, .fr and .uk for China, Germany, France and the United Kingdom respectively. In 1996, this control of domains was transferred to the US Department of Commerce which was deemed more appropriate as the Internet took on a more commercial character.

Given the special importance and global credibility of the dotcom domain, these actions tended to maintain monopoly control and extraction of rents over the issuance of domain names and over access to the so-called A-root server, which is the top-level server for running addresses by ICANN. Network Solutions, a US-based company, charged for the sale of domains to both domestic and international companies and had prices that were up to $70 which, in real terms, is five times or more the typical annual price available today for dotcom domains.

This US control of the domain system also extended to controlling the A-root server, with its database that would match enquiries to find a domain's server and would thus obtain information on the exact location where those enquires originated. This was presumably viewed, at the time, as important to supporting information gathering capabilities of the US security services, though only expressed through the US Department of Commerce's control over the apparatus. The US security establishment interest was, quite legitimately, never abandoned, as in addition to the Internet's value as a source of information about many aspects of internet users, the origins of the Internet were related to maintaining secure communication systems in case of extreme events as well as for normal confidential communications. In 2001, the ICANN president allegedly admitted that ICANN had a monopoly. After extensive pressure internationally, ICANN did add European and Asian representatives to its board by 2003.

Ultimately, the Department of Commerce control has been ceded to more international governance of the internet structure which has also allowed for the proliferation of high-level domain names. Yet the historic origins of the internet governance debate can still be seen in the fact that other countries commercial domains are one step down in the domain structure from that in the US. This means that if you want to go to Starbucks' website in the UK, it is found at Starbucks.co.uk, while if you want to go to its US website, the domain is simply starbucks.com. That is, the US does not need to use a top-level domain of ".us" for its corporate or government activities. Some countries have allowed commercial companies to effectively move one step up the chain of domain names, such as France, which does not require use of a commercial indicator in domain names and would thus allow Starbucks.fr as a domain.

The efforts by the US government to maintain control and influence over the internet architecture thus date back to the origin of the Internet. While they have turned out to benefit US companies, the structure could have benefited foreign companies as well, given that one of the objectives of the US government was to prevent control by an ungovernable and overly bureaucratic institutions like the UN, as well as to prevent other countries from designing policies that would hurt US internet businesses.

(D) Ensuring that cross-border tax rules operate to the benefit of the United States

One of the most prescient moves by the US government with respect to digital business was to guarantee it a favorable tax treatment. The US pushed for an international treaty for international taxation that did not have special conditions for digital business. This agreement was adopted by the OECD in November 2016 and named the Multilateral Convention to Implement Tax Treaty Related Measures to Prevent Base Erosion and Profit Shifting. It took effect for 99 jurisdictions in July 2018. This convention aimed for the benefit of allowing synchronized modification of bilateral tax treaties. Such changes were important because many corporate tax avoidance measures gained strength from taking advantage of multiple tax treaties. The OECD principles have also established that, to prevent moving of profits to seek special low tax jurisdictions, the default home base for taxation of multinational activities would be the productive home for the relevant activity. This provision was very much to the advantage of the large home bases of multinationals, the US, Germany and ultimately China. The US gained a position as the default home of taxation of US digital company earnings, clarifying that their profits should be taxed in the US. Remarkably, this general agreement did not have a digital exception. It was agreed to by non-US negotiators and politicians interested in short-term political gains, who were only subsequently interested in a special digital tax regime. As a result, an international baseline was established that made the US the main beneficiary of digital company profit taxes.

Efforts to modify the agreement continue running at a slow speed, as it is difficult to imagine why any country, operating in its economic self-interest, would agree to later changes that would reduce its tax take and augment that of other countries.

Normal tax treaties are negotiated with more potential for bilateral gains. A digital tax agreement in contrast will have one clear loser, since the US benefits greatly from the status quo. The fact that non-US countries agreed to such a treaty applying to digital companies shows that their tax authorities and political masters may have been more motivated by a desire for a broad step forward in corporate tax clarity, along with the political value of announcing an agreement under their watch, instead of pursuing their country's long-term economic self-interest. That is, the US success on avoiding digital tax provisions up through 2024 may be viewed simply as the result of better negotiations by the government of the United States. This superior performance may be due to long appointments of its civil servants in the same jobs, more built-in patience and more sustained strategic focus on maintaining its desired economic outcomes.

In the absence of a multilateral digital tax agreement, countries have resorted to unilaterally raising their own tax levels, on top of existing US taxes. France and Spain, for example, instigated special regimes of digital taxation in their books. Such double taxation is fundamentally unfair. While European countries try to impose sales taxes that prove that they are willing to move away from the principle of avoiding double tax, the consumer impacts of the taxes chosen were immediately problematic, because extra taxes were quite reasonably passed on by the companies affected. A special agreement has been negotiated between the US and France,

Germany, Spain and the UK, which will seek to implement a form of digital taxation arrangement.

(E) Ensuring that cross-border trade rules operate to the benefit of the United States

The share of digital production in trade flows is thought to have risen to 17 percent as of 2020. It has been one of the fastest growing areas of trade, and COVID-19 accelerated this movement.

Digital trade flows range from streaming services to online education. Zoom meetings can cross borders, as can Google search, Spotify and many other activities. Quantifying the real value of these data flows across borders and between companies can be a challenge even if transfer pricing analysis can suggest solutions.

As of October 2021, international trade agreements on e-commerce that have involved the US include a chapter of the Trans-Pacific Partnership, now part of the Comprehensive and Progressive Trans-Pacific Partnership from 2016; a chapter of the US-Mexico-Canada Agreement from 2019; and the US-Japan Digital Trade Agreement of 2019.

The types of activities covered by digital agreements apply to international digital movements, such as data flows, digital communications, and access to websites. The agreements permit exceptions to open trade for reasons of public order, morals and national security. These exceptions could be interpreted quite broadly. In addition, the agreements could have binding arbitration between signatories in case of disagreement between signatory countries.

These agreements include so-called "good housekeeping" provisions. These suggest that customs duties would not be applied to electronic transmissions, digital products will not receive "discriminatory treatment," and enablement of electronic signatures and authentication. In addition, the agreements call for prohibiting fraudulent and deceptive digital activity as well as ensuring protections for personal digital data.

A more significant agreement would be a broader international one that would encompass developed and developing countries. As of 2022, such an agreement was under discussion with the WTO's E-Commerce Joint Statement Initiative. 71 of the 164 WTO members have been engaged in the discussions, including China, the EU, Japan, the UK and the US. A rough version of the agreement was released by the WTO in December 2020, but this release was heavily commented by individual members. Experts at the Peterson Institute for International Economics suggest that the fundamental differences between some of the 71 parties will make an ambitious agreement unlikely.

The revised US-Mexico-Canada Trade Agreement (USMCTA), which replaced NAFTA under the Trump administration, reveals the three main concerns of the US. The first is ensuring that digital platforms would not be liable for third-party content. The second is that digital platforms would be free to delete postings by third parties. And the third is that any digital service taxes should not discriminate against US companies. One may expect that the first feature will not be accepted by many countries. In a remarkable forcing of private companies to take on policing powers, governments are requiring that ensure appropriateness of their content. A company that fails to take steps that ensure appropriateness will be subject to liability.

The Peterson Institute suggests that Chinese demands for an agreement may be well reflected in Asia's Regional Comprehensive Economic Partnership. In this agreement to which China has adhered, China allows for several key rights of the country receiving data. The first permits a requirement to localize computing facilities like cloud computing within a country. The second permits restricting data flows from foreign countries for services and investment. The third allows a signatory to require disclosure of software source code as a precondition for an internet company to operate in a country. Prohibitions of tariff duties on electronic transmissions are allowed in case the WTO Ministerial Decisions forbidding such duties are not renewed. In case of disagreements between members, the possibility of arbitration is not provided, but rather a basic requirement to enter good faith negotiations.

This Ministerial Declaration is less permanent than a formal treaty because the declaration must be renewed to keep in force. Yet its continual renewal shows how the original prohibition of tariffs on electronic transmissions, first endorsed by the WTO in 1998, has meant that tariffs are not applied to digital sales, despite reported hesitations from countries like South Africa. The WTO's Ambassador from Japan "noted that 65 members have put forward a proposal to renew the multilateral moratorium on the imposition of customs duties on e-commerce" reported by the WTO update. While many individual companies in a variety of countries benefit from such a moratorium, the largest beneficiary country in aggregate is the US. This lopsided gain from avoiding digital tariffs explains why even under the generally WTO-skeptical Trump administration, the electronic commerce discussion at the WTO was a clear priority for the US. In a victory for US internet companies, this moratorium on customs duties for e-commerce was again renewed in June 2022.

8. THE FUTURE ALONG THE CURRENT PATH

All's fair in love and war.
-Francis Edward Smedley

If nothing fundamentally changes, where will this internet domination end? It is worth noting that consumer purchases over the internet have been increasing at a rate of 20 percent per year, meaning that, if this continues, over 5 years, the amount purchased over the Internet would more than double, increasing by 150 percent. There are inevitably limits to the extent to which the internet companies can grow, as some business will always remain local. However, we can expect continuing closures of some storefronts, as internet companies offer increasingly fast home delivery and improved customization of products. Traditional companies that survive will be agile and adaptable, needing to respond quickly and aggressively in function of where internet companies are hurting their business.

Meanwhile, internet-based platforms will increase their market share and increase their control over purchasing transactions and sharing of information.

Moving from advertising to transactional model

Google and other search engines can increase their ability to monetize searches, by monitoring buying patterns that arise from clicks and by developing innovative methods of turning searches into sales, as well as expanding the set of products they sell directly.

As search engines or other platforms become our link to discovering information about the world, the platforms will find increasingly creative ways to extract the value from generated transactions.

Google, in 2019, introduced a new method for companies to pay for search, in which instead of paying Google by click they would pay Google by sale. The condition of this is to let Google observe the sales process for customers they would bring to a company.

As Google obtains a better understanding of which sales come from their customers, they may well demand a better percentage of the markup on each customer. In effect, Google could move from being an advertising medium to a virtual salesperson that effectively earns a high commission on each item sold. The company could credibly threaten to move sales to other sellers if they do not receive a high commission for sales.

This transactional aspiration has been seen in efforts of Google to start running its own shopping comparison services. If it improves and gains good understanding of how to make sales happen, it can seek to take over these transactions. It may use this power, in part, to reduce the market power of other platforms. For example, TripAdvisor has become a trusted source of evaluations of restaurant and hotel options, particularly for US customers. However, Google has started showing its own ratings for restaurants and hotels, increasingly performing this valuable service without having the same hidden (to the consumer) charges that other companies might have.

Not only will advertising move towards transactions, but some marketplaces may move towards product creation. While Amazon has been accused of copying products from successful sellers and is under investigation by the European Commission for self-preferencing, there is a fundamental potential innovative strength in its search activities: Amazon can learn about products that are in demand but not being supplied. It can then start making them. In one small example of this sort, I searched for a tool bag on Amazon that would be just large enough to hold a hacksaw that I bought, but not any larger. Weirdly, the bags that were available on its marketplace were all substantially too small or too large for the type of saw I had bought.

Months later, I went back again to look at tool bags on Amazon. This time, there was a tool bag available, of exactly the design I wanted and exactly the size. It was made by Amazon. Evidently, by comparing with what was available in other marketplaces or reviewing its own search records, Amazon might have determined that many people wanted a bag of the same, unserved size. Their knowledge that there was a gap in their own marketplace presumably led them to fill that gap themselves. In fact, more than 85 percent of Amazon-created products are introduced to fill unserved gaps that the company has identified. The creation of new products to fill gaps is another trend that will follow from the internet companies increased knowledge of our wants and demands. Such a creation will deliver valuable consumer surplus.

The future activities of Google and other large internet companies remain difficult to predict. Will Google use its power over search to become, increasingly, a direct seller of goods and services? In doing so, would it raise commission levels, or would it create competition with existing sellers? To the extent that serving as a direct seller is feasible, the change would be very much in its interest. For example, arguably, Google could sell airline tickets, hotel nights and museum entry passes just as well as the specialized platforms. Google could sell insurance and banking products taking advantage of the high level of consumer trust in the company. Could Google sell cars?

Delivery will continue to substitute for in person stores

Delivery businesses have evolved in amazing ways over the last two decades. This evolution will likely continue, as internet sellers grow closer to consumers and overcome barriers to delivery, such as people not being home when a delivery person arrives.

Some reminders are useful to have a sense of what has happened in that evolution. First, twenty years ago, all delivery of goods by major e-retailers typically used the very large delivery services, like Fedex, UPS, and DHL and the national postal carriers. Delivery would typically take days, even when the item purchased was in stock at the seller. Now, internet retailers have built out their storage facilities to be increasingly close to consumers, they have increasingly hired their own delivery service people, whether as employees or independent contractors. Sometimes, they use intermediaries to manage storage facilities, which can reduce claims from unions that large marketplaces were imposing unfair conditions on workers. Amazon invented the idea of having supervisors walk the walkway above the storage shelves to ensure that workers are working. They also invented the idea of having daily challenges, with an objective for each employee to beat their prior productivity levels every day.

Now, many products are deliverable within hours. Fresh food delivery from multiple restaurateurs has become the rage, especially as people start to regard ordering food to their house as one of the normal ways of getting food. Lockers for delivery of goods are also available at indoor and outdoor locations. These ensure delivery of goods can occur at all times of the day even when people are working away from home or out for the day. Interestingly, historic postal operators which once had the lead on mailboxes have failed to innovate and find new high passage locations for large "mailbox" lockers that, due to electronic codes, can change users from hour to hour and day to day. The presence of delivery lockers illustrates the benefits of companies like Amazon creating genuinely useful innovation that prior delivery companies had failed to imagine and implement.

While local delivery provided a remarkable source of new jobs for people whose work was displaced by Covid-19 and associated lockdowns, the changing nature of delivery may have meant that those who in the past might have driven long-distance trucks increasingly prefer to deliver short-distance goods, creating a scarcity of truck drivers.

If delivery by drone becomes widely accepted by people and governments, the efficiency of the delivery process could increase, along with the accuracy of leaving packages in the right place and at a pre-arranged hour. But drones could reduce the need for delivery people to carry such packages.

Ownership of key platforms will create further concentration in the ownership of customer relationships

The so-called elimination of intermediaries that economists and internet gurus predicted for the internet back in 2000 has been proven definitively wrong. The prediction was that the Internet would allow people to find and buy directly from producers, eliminating the need for sellers in the middle.

In practice, while the number of small sellers may have increased in many domains, from t-shirts to ceramics, thanks to platforms like Etsy or Amazon, the importance of intermediaries for sales has only grown.

Decentralization on the Internet has been followed by a massive recentralization. One of the reasons for this is that the Internet makes an enormous amount of information available. Many of its early users hoped to facilitate direct information exchange without the need for any central organization. The lowering of the cost of search was viewed as a way to tame monopoly power that might exist. But ironically, the high volume of information available, and its imperfect quality, makes finding the right information difficult for individual users. We have natural constraints on our time, information processing power and memory. These constraints lead us to prefer external information processing centers, such as search engines or rating websites or electronic catalogs, over reconstructing the information from scratch. This means that, due to the constraints and costs of personal processing of information, information is recentralized externally. This centralization is perhaps inevitable but can also create power that can potentially be misused.

The percentage of people picking up a phone and booking their hotel rooms directly has dramatically fallen. In the past, guides issued by chains showed the locations and phone numbers of that chain's hotels. This may have given chains an advantage over independent hotels, which had difficulty being discovered. Now, the use of printed travel guides to find hotels has declined. But the core challenge of finding a room in unknown places remains. Increasingly people go to intermediaries like Booking.com and Expedia to find and book their hotel rooms. While the exact market share of such services is difficult to know, it may be that as much as 50 percent of hotel sales occur through these services.

These services buy keyword advertising from search engines both by hotel name and by city name to appear at the top of the first search page. Individual hotels and even chains have a hard time competing with the price that an online travel agency is willing to pay for a click. Indeed, the value of advertising is much greater for these services than for individual hotels for two reasons. First, online hotel booking services offer a large panel of hotels to their client. Therefore, the likelihood of translating a click into a purchase is higher for companies like Booking.com than for independent hotels. Second, these services increasingly try to retain consumers, to entice them to use their services repeatedly, using loyalty programs and personalized recommendations. If a lone hotel gets a click, it may at best get the client to purchase a stay and perhaps come back in the future. Booking.com however could gain a loyal consumer which will use its services for most of their hotel searches across many cities. The online booking services convert their high commissions into discounts for subsequent stays, while essentially requiring that online prices of hotels cannot be discounted compared to their own rack rate, prior to the giving of a loyalty rebate.

New brick-and-mortar models will develop

Brick-and-mortar store activity will change in at least two ways. The first occurs as existing stores expand into the Internet. The second occurs as internet sellers expand into brick-and-mortar stores.

Among the first category, brick-and-mortar businesses will increasingly expand into the Internet. Many businesses have opened a website or use a third-party marketplace to advertise their catalogue online, and offer delivery services or use their stores for click and collect. The way they expand will affect the future geography of the Internet, as they may choose to run their own websites, become suppliers on another marketplace or both. A sports goods chain may serve as a brand aggregator and massively increase the selection of running shoes and sizes that it can sell when doing so online. Furthermore, the shoe brands themselves may introduce online stores. These stores can add new innovations that create hitherto unseen products. Shoe providers, such as

Converse, are now offering the possibility to design your own pair of shoes, with particular colors of uppers, tongues and shoelaces.

Large supermarkets have adapted to the idea of having consumers order their groceries online and either doing a click and collect, in which the consumer picks up at the store, or having the goods delivered direct to the consumer residence.

On another front, it is worth recognizing that the largest internet retailer is proving through its own actions that it fundamentally believes in the future of stores. Amazon which many people once thought of as an internet retailer does not consider itself constrained in this way. Rather, it is showing particularly innovative approaches to expanding its retail presence, notably with the acquisition of Whole Foods Market, that brings it into new domains. The acquisition allegedly allowed Amazon to use its negotiating savvy to lower its own costs while serving a group of customers that are less price sensitive than in other grocery chains. In some markets, it has rolled out Amazon Fresh, a new store model that was introduced in the Los Angeles suburb of Woodland Hills in 2020, after years of Amazon trialing and perfecting the technology. This store rolled out the innovative concept of self-check-out using sensor and video technology to learn the goods in your shopping basket and to avoid the need to scan them.

Retail and other jobs will disappear

The internet sales phenomenon, which has been so well accepted by the youngest generation of consumers, but also by most other consumers, including the elderly and those who have difficulty getting to stores, is fundamentally changing the volume of sales that go to brick-and-mortar retail stores. The economic consequence of lost sales to brick-and-mortar stores is that their revenues per store are likely to go down, if they keep the same number of stores and the same selection.

Lost revenues translate directly into reduced employment in stores that survive or reduction in the number of stores in a chain. Some jobs that have been lost from retail have been replaced, for the moment, by more jobs in delivery. This is particularly the case because ordering goods individually is, in many instances, less efficient than having stores order the goods and us picking up a variety of goods in the store.

As more and more books were ordered over the Internet, more bookstores have been closed around the world. Many bookshop owners have had to retrain and change career, to one that they may enjoy less.

Similarly, as advertising has increasingly moved online, newspapers are finding it difficult to raise revenue, and employ the same number of journalists. News and specialty journalists lost jobs and the salaries of those remaining have not kept up. The quality of news consumed by typical users has fallen, due to the increased consumer reliance on journalistic sources that might include fake news.

Consumers themselves will move rapidly into new niches

Consumers have become increasingly open to engaging in new ways of purchasing and new forms of buying. For example, consumers have been willing to use companies that offer forms of orthodontic services online, like tooth straightening devices from SmileDirect. This company provides consumers with a way to make a cast of their teeth from home, and then ships them teeth straightening inserts that are changed every two weeks to give a better and better alignment of teeth.

Similarly, basic hearing aids will increasingly be available from mass merchandisers or via internet delivery. Such hearing aids may reduce the costs of a new hearing aid substantially while still allowing some customization of hearing aids to the needs of a user. The price difference for such products can mean that millions of people who would not otherwise have afforded hearing aids may now be able to access such essential products.

This is not to suggest the quality of such new services is always the same in all respects as that which occurs from human delivered services. But at the same time, such services make products available that were otherwise much more expensive and out of the reach of ordinary citizens.

9. CLASSIC WAR DEFENSES

To be always ready for war, said Mentor, is the surest way to avoid it.
-François de Salignac de la Mothe Fénelon

This book has argued that the territorial expansion enabled by the Internet has, in its economic consequences, resembled the outcome of war. What has not been so far discussed is how to respond. If there is no problem with the takeover, and it is purely an example of innovation winning out over prior technologies, no response may be necessary. In contrast, if there is a problem with this internet takeover responses may be needed. Certainly, many non-US governments consider that there might be a problem with the US supremacy over their digital economy, and many users and politicians across the world have expressed concerns. What are the options for response? One set of useful ideas could come from prior experience of how to defend against a classic war. While the analogy of war defense is far from perfect, because the means of the territorial takeover are quite distinct, we can distil some broad conclusions and ideas for response from prior experience with defense against war.

If the takeover of the internet world is an economic war, and if this is a problem, then countries and their citizens who wish to "defend" themselves may reasonably ask how to do so. Some of the classic defenses from the past may be adapted. So we will first focus on existing defensive strategies. Subsequent, we will show how these historical forms of defense can be adapted, and emphasize that in the case of the Internet we would benefit from much more focused attention to *individual* in addition to *government* decision making. The appropriate changes to individual behavior will depend on (1) the exact nature of the concerns arising from the Internet, and (2) ways to address these concerns without creating consequences that are worse than the original problem.

The overt hostility of conquered populations arising from traditional violence and the force of war and empire building may be irrelevant. The internet takeover is occurring peacefully through technological diffusion of innovation at a faster pace than at any time in history. Compared to traditional methods of defense, new and more sophisticated defenses may be needed in place of the traditional blunt tools. Identifying the best ones is a hard task for politicians and policy makers. The challenge is to find appropriate solutions that will allow citizens to continue benefitting from high quality services while preventing any insidious effects from the dominance and empire building of internet companies.

Classic war defenses can be divided into four major categories, establishing border defenses, counterattacking, building alliances to dissuade potential attackers and improving technical capabilities of the forces in battle.

Barriers

The most classic war defense is illustrated in ancient and medieval cities. At the time, cities were places of relative security, surrounded by high walls that could be defended easily in case of attack. In medieval Europe, the rate of murder was roughly ten times that of today. Travel and trade were unsafe, as thieves and brigands would wait besides country roads to rob travelers and merchants. In addition, small gangs would attack rural outposts, and hostile neighbors could conduct lightning raids on border towns. But valuables such as grain would be stored in cities which were protected by walls that would resist fire and battering rams, and often located on defensive positions such as hills.

On some occasions, substantial border protections were put in place. The most impressive defensive structure is the Great Wall of China. It defended the northern borders of ancient Chinese states and Imperial China, extending for about 3,080 km under the Qin and Han dynasties and extended to 8,850 km under the Ming. The wall was built for preventing attacks by marauders from the northern steppes beyond China.

In ports, barriers were often installed as well. For example, in Constantinople a long iron chain was set across the Golden Horn, controlling a major inlet that would provide access for an attack at the weakly defended back of the city. This was first installed in 717 AD and used as part of a trap to stop an overwhelming waterborne attack by forces of the Umayyad Caliphate. The great chain continued to defend the city for centuries, and even helped the ultimately unsuccessful defense of the city in the year 1453 when it fell to the attack of forces of Sultan Mehmed II.

In more modern times, nets were installed across entries to some ports during World War II, such as Sydney Harbor or Scotland's Clyde Estuary, to prevent enemy ships and submarines from wreaking havoc on moored ships.

Anti-personnel mines have been an important element of defense in recent times, as an effective substitute for maintaining a costly permanent sentry armed presence to guard an area which, while effective in daytime, may fail to detect intruders at night. Mines are a combination of a sensor of presence (such as a compression sensor when someone steps on them) and an explosive. Mines, buried in the ground, can serve not only to provide a protection to open borders, but also larger ones can disable transports (on unsurfaced roads, for example) or ships. Mines can create invisible barriers, while allowing those with a good map to pass through an area unharmed. Whether terrestrial or water-based, mines are economically effective means of defense, due to the reduced need for human sentries, and thus can be considered, from an economic perspective, as a cost reducing form for boundary protection both for defenders.

Counterattack: The best defense is a strong offense

An alternative feature of defense is the ability and willingness to attack. The ability of a defender to counterattack can force opponents to reduce their initial attacking forces, or even prevent an attack in the first place.

One classic example of counterattack comes from Roman times. The core of the Roman Empire was under attack by the brilliant general Hannibal in 217 BC, during the Second Punic War, who created surprise by crossing the mountains into the North of Italy with an army that included elephants. He and his army were from the Phoenician trading empire, based in Carthage, a city on the southern Mediterranean in modern-day Tunisia. While the Romans suffered defeat after defeat by Hannibal's army, as he slowly marched his warriors and elephants towards Rome, the Romans were able to send legions south across the Mediterranean, to attack the city of Carthage. Under threat in his own capital, Hannibal ultimately had to abandon his attacks on Italy to retreat and defend Carthage. The Roman ability to attack Carthage and carry an army by ship across the Mediterranean meant that, even though Roman cities were falling under attack, they could attack the base of their attacker, forcing him to return home before achieving his objective of conquering Rome.

Alliances

One of the best defenses in time of prospective war is to form alliances, often in the form of mutual defense treaties.

At the outbreak of World War II, Poland had treaties for mutual defense with other European countries. These included a longstanding mutual assistance agreement with France dating from 1921. They also included a new one with Great Britain dating from 6 April 1939, signed in the shadows of the ongoing German military buildup. The September 1939 German-Soviet Union attack on Poland thus created a much broader allied response. Due to Poland's alliances, Britain and France immediately declared war on Germany.

After World War II, during the Cold War period, the NATO alliance played a key role as a deterrent to USSR military intervention worldwide, and especially in Europe. The NATO alliance provides mutual guarantees of security between its members. It is one of the most integrated military alliances in history, as it created a formal control mechanism with a headquarters, a permanent joint command system, and regular joint training of its constituent armies. The headquarters has its own staff, civil service and retirement system. It survived through difficulties in its own management, such as when France pulled out of NATO in 1966, and became a simple coordinating partner, rather than a member of the organization. Joint exercises, communications networks and joint deployments to existing war zones have ensured that the organization has the capability to respond without relying on political agreements being formed after an attack takes place.

Arming the people

One defense against attack is to arm the citizens so that any attacker, whichever direction they face, will find potential danger. Arming citizens can take a variety of forms, from giving them guns, to permitting them to carry guns, to training them in the use of weapons and resistance.

This approach was explicitly part of the Constitution of the United States, which guaranteed a right to bear arms, to ensure its citizens could battle any foreign power that might wish to insert itself into the United States. While the constitutional protection of bearing arms is much maligned, it must be seen in its original context, as the United States emerged from the first revolution against British power, with Britain still present on the northern border in Canada. This posed a real risk of future battle and invasion, which materialized as the British took Washington DC and burned down the original White House in 1814. Taking Washington DC was not enough to take control of the former rebel states, however, and with an appropriate treaty in place, the British retreated.

The Swiss have a tradition of training and arming its citizens to protect its long history of independence. The Swiss send all young citizens to military training and, upon the conclusion of that training, provide them with rifles, uniforms and communications gear so that a decentralized resistance can be started and maintained against any foreign incursion and so that reserve military units can be formed quickly throughout the country. Even in World War II, the Swiss managed to remain independent, while surrounded by German-controlled powers. This remarkable achievement may come in part from diplomacy, but also from non-alignment with alliances that would have been counter to any aggressive power.

Israel also requires military service. The Israeli concern arises from being surrounded on many sides by countries that have questioned its right to exist. Israel has been involved in multiple wars, including the 1956 Sinai invasion, June 1967 Arab-Israeli War, the October 1973 Arab-Israeli War, and the 1982 and 2002 Lebanon Wars. Upon leaving the Israeli army, citizens are issued with military equipment and drafted into the reserves, so that they can be called to the army at a moment's notice.

The Roman empire's strategy of giving land in the newly conquered territories to retired legionnaires served the purpose of ensuring it would have local defenders across its lands. The bonus land spread the military strength of Rome into the new settlements, and created local warriors ready to support the Roman Empire against incursion or rebellion.

These examples are not meant to suggest, by analogy, ways for other countries to address the internet war. The approaches taken are not presented with a positive or negative value judgement. Rather, they illustrate the principle that countries under attack may choose to arm their citizens. Strategically, this approach can make sense and, whatever debates may surround the practice, military readiness of the people can be a powerful instrument to reduce the willingness of external parties to attack.

One of the fundamental techniques of defense in time of war is thus built on individual action that is bottom-up rather than top-down.

Individual action, carried out simultaneously by a large and uncoordinated group, can prevent the attainment of military objectives and raise the costs of military incursion to unacceptable levels for an invader. Coordination of such individual action will make the impacts of that action even stronger.

These response strategies show that the first line of defense for a geography under attack is government response. This includes barriers, counterattack and simple defense, as well as coordinating responses against the attacker. But the response can also include individual action, by arming the citizens and relying on them to fight back and change the calculation of benefits and costs of takeover for the attacker.

The government responses can thus be to create physical

barriers, create military dissuasion through centralized armed forces and to create diplomatic dissuasion via alliances, which are designed to augment the defensive power of individual countries.

Slowly, many of these government responses are emerging against the Internet Empire. Governments are taking actions to limit the power of internet companies over their economies and, even in the US, government is limiting the commercial power of internet companies, as with activities by its law enforcement authorities under antitrust laws, which include cases against Amazon, Meta (Facebook) and Alphabet (Google) at the time of writing, and may extend to further laws in the future. So far, though, only China and Russia have created direct barriers to takeover by foreign internet companies, which are the Internet equivalent to physical barriers of defense.

In addition to government responses, many takeovers see an important role played by citizens as resistance fighters. The analogy for the Internet Empire would not involve giving citizens guns or organizing a violent resistance. Rather, the analogy would be through citizens changing the way they act, and taking advantage of flexibilities provided by law to ensure that internet power is constrained and has less problematic social consequences. Individual action is thus a key and much neglected aspect of responding to the takeover by the Internet Empire.

With these points in mind, we will move on to consider how governments and individuals can respond. For government responses, the precise question is: what can governments do about the internet companies? Can the governments build barriers and counterattack?

10. POSSIBLE GOVERNMENT RESPONSES

War is not merely a political act, but also a political instrument, a continuation of political relations, carrying out the same by other means.
-Karl von Clausewitz

The cat in gloves catches no mice.
-Benjamin Franklin

For the moment, most governments have accepted the US companies' takeover of a large portion of their economic activity. They have not desired this takeover, but they have also not acted as if a war had been engaged against them. Just as it is difficult to realize that a remarkable virtual war has taken place, it is difficult for non-US governments to treat the winners as aggressors. It is especially difficult to respond harshly to this takeover since it has been orchestrated peacefully by numerous private companies, rather than by one united invader.

The US Government support in this endeavor has been inherently limited. The frontline is run by multinational internet companies. Moreover, from the perspective of foreign countries, many of the ill effects they are concerned about apply equally to US citizens who have also at times suffered from negative impacts of their internet companies.

Thus, the US companies are not treating US customers any better than those elsewhere.

Most governments can take comfort from the fact that they do still control their borders. They can adopt the classic responses to foreign aggression that were the focus of the previous chapter, but they should be adapted to the new method of territorial expansion. They could theoretically require filters at central internet backbone points that stop the activity of foreign companies who are operating in their land. The digital form of an ancient stone could potentially protect some countries from the internet takeover. For example, if a government felt that insufficient taxes were being paid, they could simply cut off the future revenue sources of the offending companies, by closing the consumer avenues of reaching their services via filters. Treaties that the US is championing on the international scene would prevent any such action and effectively take away the most fundamental tool that is available to non-US governments. However, even without this requirement, most governments would be reluctant to limit access of their citizens to large internet companies due to the popularity of the services with citizens.

If "walls" are not built, government responses would need to be targeted at different types of problems. We next consider some of the problems and narrow-based and broad-based solutions to those problems.

Social dis-hesion

The direct political threat of individualized advertising over the Internet was highlighted in the Cambridge Analytica allegations concerning the 2016 US election. In this incident, personal information was allegedly used for advertising that would target and change votes for individuals in a way that would influence election outcomes. Whether this attitude influencing effort was successful or not, the core concern is much more general, arising from the combination of the democratic liberty of advertising in elections and the increased possibility to customize advertising to individuals. The political manipulation threat posed by the Internet needs to be addressed urgently, due to its potentially existential threat to democracy. However, a much more subtle but equally damaging effect of the Internet is to create self-reinforcing belief systems.

The tradition of democratic countries with common visions of the world, a tradition that may have reached its zenith in the 1990s, has since drastically declined. Social dis-hesion (as opposed to adhesion) is arising out of the segmentation of interests. Prior to the advent of the Internet, news consumers could choose one media over another because of its political alignment. But the relatively small number of broadly accessed print and radio media tended to follow standards of neutrality and objectivity, and offered a relatively diverse range of opinions and content. Television, especially in its early days when only a handful of channels were available, was perhaps the most universal media. The small number of channels with high viewership may be directly responsible for the high level of social cohesion that became the hallmark of 1990s democracies. In the 1990s, most citizens spent 4-5 hours per day watching television. This was like injecting a unified, tranquilizing drug to the masses. In France, 80 percent of evening television watchers drew their news from one common source, the private TF1 news service. Today the source of news has changed. Many of us now get our news from the Internet. Not only do we use many different sources, preventing social cohesion, but much of this news is produced by politically oriented services do not follow all journalistic standards.

Internet viewers are delivered highly personalized content, content that will keep them on the platform and thus generate higher revenue. Therefore, rather than gaining access to a rich and diverse web of information, users are fed content which tends to confirm their existing beliefs and biases. If the most profitable options are those that confirm biases, which seems to be the case, the right, the left and other political persuasions will tend to separate into distinct groups that increasingly do not share a common factual basis nor a common value system for looking at the world.

Platforms could be under an obligation to provide the best information possible, in a way that is politically unbiased, thus preventing social dis-hesion.

Platforms could be responsible for policing the quality of information and material on their platform, with an affirmative obligation to prevent distribution of false news. The societal consequences of fake news can be substantial not only for exaggerating the dis-hesion but also for influencing outcomes of democratic elections. For example, the Cambridge Analytica data was allegedly used for targeting and influencing voters considered likely to change their votes on politicians or major political developments such as Brexit.

Platforms may reasonably object that they are not able to police information. The practical ability for them to oversee quality of information is simply impracticable without a drastic change in their business model and a dramatic limitation on freedom of speech. A recent decision in Australia applied to Facebook this principle of an obligation to privately police the Internet. Such decisions create enormous uncertainty for Facebook even as Facebook devotes high resources to trying to stop the problematic material. Such rules may stifle free expression of views.

The problem is a dual problem of platforms allowing highly divergent views of the world to be presented and the customization of information to different categories of people so that views on public policy diverge.

Platforms may also be restricted in the extent to which they can offer personalized content of a political nature. It could even be required that news information be presented to users without considering their identity or history. Only if we once again attain a common perspective on the world, and see our perspectives challenged by central tendencies, will we be able to have effective democracy with a bulk of people in the center with moderate views.

Merger policy

Many digital mergers have not been reviewed due to the nature of thresholds that exclude "small revenue value" deals from being reviewed. But internet companies' strategy of acquiring all the promising new digital start-ups nips future competition in the bud.

When acquirers pay billions of dollars more than is justified by the current profitability of their target, the payment itself suggests anti-competitive effect. But often such deals have not been reviewed. The way that competition agencies view thresholds for review and even evaluation of effects clearly needs revision. Competition authorities would typically focus on the actual revenues of the firms. If the acquired firm is bought for a price in the billions but has no revenue, the transaction would typically not be captured by the traditional minimum commerce thresholds that were designed to ensure that small mergers were not subject to investigation and the following intervention by competition authorities. One principle underlying the merger review process is that no company has a right to buy out its future opposition. Permitting such buyouts creates a distortion of the competitive market process.

While formal figures are not released, there are estimates that Google and other top internet companies, for example, have acquired 500 companies in the last 10 years. Only a few of these deals have been seriously reviewed and none have been stopped until 2021.

The absence of a careful review of merger deals happens in many different sectors. For example, a number of long-distance bus company mergers took place in France after the long-distance busing industry experienced substantial entry around 2014-15, based around sales over digital apps. None of these deals were subject to merger review, because of the ownership structure of the bus companies, in which many small operators delivered the service under a common brand. The result was that acquisitions were excluded from review by the merger review minimum size thresholds.

In the lightest version of what governments can do for the Internet, they could accept that we are in an age of industrial reconfiguration and that mergers involving digital companies are at the core of creating the enterprises of tomorrow. Reviewing acquisitions based on minimum revenue thresholds may in that case be fine, because one desires the reconfiguring of industry that is inevitable.

Venture capitalists consider the possibility of their investment being bought by one of the large internet companies as one of the best potential ways to exit an investment. At the same time, venture capitalists are worried about having so few buyers competing for the young enterprises they help to create. Moreover, they are unlikely to invest in activities that directly take on an established player.

Governments may wish to implement stronger policies to support merger intervention. In the strongest version of what governments may wish to consider, dominant internet companies would simply be banned from acquiring and investing in others, but only permitted to grow organically. Such an approach seems extreme. It is not well focused because less than 5 percent of mergers have been argued as problematic.

An alternative approach is to seek spinoffs of mergers that are later deemed problematic. For example, Facebook acquired two social networks, WhatsApp in 2014 and Instagram in 2012. No competition authority challenged these until the US FTC in 2020 sued, in an extraordinary and atypical fashion, for the unscrambling of Facebook's merger with WhatsApp and Instagram. Such challenges are rare under competition law in part because of the difficulty of "unscrambling the eggs" after a merger has been already completed. Furthermore, such post-merger intervention can penalize the companies that have undertaken these acquisitions in a way that creates excessive ambiguity about which deals are legal and which ones are not.

Another problem with post-merger "unscrambling" is that the prosecutions are highly selective. Already at the time of these mergers, many people felt that there was a systemic threat being posed by these systematic acquisitions of new entrants. When Google acquired the travel application Waze, some observers noted that it already had the most advanced mapping and driving solution, one that could already offer most of the services of Waze. The acquisition thus did not appear aimed to add new innovative technology. An alternative explanation was that the acquisition would secure greater market power or prevent other companies from getting better mapping solutions. Yet Google (via Motorola Mobility) was allowed to acquire the competitive mapping company without facing any challenge. Only the UK competition authority intervened with an investigation, but it ultimately issued a decision that allowed the merger to proceed. No authority has sought to undo this merger.

We can legitimately ask whether Google and Facebook would be facing more competition if another company had been allowed to form an alternative behemoth that included, for example, Waze, WhatsApp and Instagram.

The best approach is to block problematic deals before they are finalized. But when this is done, the right deals must be selected. Selecting them requires a well-honed ability to predict the future. The first true internet deal to be blocked by government was the purchase by Facebook of Giphy. This acquisition was declared incompatible with the competition law by the UK competition authority in 2021. Giphy is a maker of GIFs and was alleged to control the developing GIF standards. Observers might wonder about the overall importance of keeping Giphy away from Meta. Courts will ultimately determine the outcome of this transaction.

What standards are then appropriate to review a merger involving digital companies? Having a standard that simply says a small subset of companies cannot make acquisitions unless they prove a net benefit to citizens is one possibility. But this approach treats some companies differently from others, without there being a principle underlying that differential treatment. Moreover, the majority of mergers are not likely to create substantial harm. Of the more than 500 digital deals that have occurred, only about 5-10 have been alleged as highly problematic. It is these 5-10 that might have been stopped, rather than all acquisitions by large internet companies.

To identify such risky mergers, the revenue threshold standard could be supplemented by a threshold ratio of acquisition price to revenue or a threshold ratio of acquisition price to employees, as noted by Kühn. Acquisitions with a ratio above the threshold would receive a more detailed review or include a changed burden of proof, with companies having to show that the merger is not harmful to competition. But the vast majority of unproblematic acquisitions would not need to be reviewed.

Another proposal has been to require merging parties to prove that their mergers do not harm competition rather than requiring the government to prove that mergers harm competition. This idea of changing which side has the burden of proof would move the burden from the government to the acquiring company, but may face due process critiques. Such a reversal would produce a system that is like giving citizens the obligation to prove they have not violated the law.

Competition authorities, though now more active in reviewing digital mergers than in the past, have singularly failed to show vision and may face severe uphill battles in courts to prove that acquisition of small new start-ups pose a challenge to competition. But if the burden of proof changes, well-intentioned competition authorities will be given broad powers to stop deals. These blockages could occur without compelling evidence in their favor and without full procedural rights of challenge. If so, they could start to misuse their newfound power, and push it to its limits. To the extent that the prosecutors have seemed incapable of dealing with mergers that build up ecosystems in new and original ways, the appropriate approach towards such mergers remains complex.

Data, privacy and market breakdown

Remarkably, the collection of extensive information on users by internet companies can lead existing markets to break down. Such a breakdown may not be a socially desirable outcome. Furthermore, the invasion of privacy entailed by the mass collection of user information may be undesirable in itself.

In 2021 Google completed its acquisition of Fitbit, the main watch-based fitness device. This merger was not challenged on the grounds that Fitbit had many competitors. The business plan of Google was not revealed, but it may be that Google wishes to use the information on users generated by Fitbit to support its other businesses. For example, it would provide Google with better information than other life insurance companies on the market about the health risks of customers. In an environment in which risks cannot be observed, insurance pools the risk of individuals with different risk profiles. Insurance is only profitable if it is sold to both high and low risk consumers. In effect, low risk individuals subsidize higher risk individuals. If Google has access to much better information than traditional life insurers, it could sell insurance only to the lower risk consumers at a competitive price, and leave higher risk consumers for the other companies. Traditional life insurance would no longer be profitable at previous prices, and this could lead to an unraveling of the market.

In South Africa, one insurer offered lower car insurance rates to drivers who use an app that enables monitoring of their driving behavior. Low-risk behavior, such as driving at or below the speed limit, making few sudden turns and no sudden stops, would result in lower premiums. Those with more dangerous driving habits and those who refused to be monitored would receive higher premiums. As in the example with Fitbit, this additional information would allow the insurance company to determine the risk profile of individuals which may lead the market to unravel but may also create incentives for individuals to adopt low-risk behavior.

Such monitoring may be considered an invasion of normal expectations of privacy. As markets drive the elimination of privacy, an enormous increase in monitoring of individual behavior is likely.

Monitoring in the future will be based on new ways to assemble and create data. At times, this may yield socially beneficial consequences, but even so may still be highly controversial, as it depends on how the data from monitoring is evaluated and the personal consequences that follow from such monitoring.

The result of increased monitoring is that our personal self-determination and freedoms to behave as one chooses may be reduced by an oversight culture that slowly envelopes us. Government may have a role in overseeing the nature of private monitoring, to ensure that desirable markets do not fall apart, and may also need to constrain itself to avoid creating a culture of constant oversight when citizens value privacy.

Control of contracting practices

Initially, policy makers thought the Internet was a great democratizing medium, making direct sales from producers to consumers much more likely. Instead, intermediaries have come to dominate the access to producers. Internet search engines, hotel booking services, airline booking services all have substantial influence over the options that are shown to consumers and can obtain what we can call monopoly intermediation margins, usually at the expense of the producers. These margins are going to the winners of the war. Governments should find routes to generally encourage or mandate that direct sales channels receive high visibility.

The contracts that dominant internet companies, and aspiring dominant companies, put in place are crucial for preventing competition over their commissions. As all users of services know, the contracts that are set in place give customers very few real options. If you want to use a software, that you need, you must say yes and accept all the terms and conditions of use. Negotiating individual contracts would be impracticable, and hence there is little real control for the users over the terms of contracts.

Two types of contracts raise particular concern:

(1)   Exclusivity: suppliers are not allowed to use rival platforms;

(2)   Price guarantees: suppliers cannot charge a lower price than that they advertise on the platform.

Exclusivity. One example of implicit exclusivity contracts comes from Uber. Uber drivers, though typically independent contractors, are provided with many incentives to operate primarily with Uber. It has been reported that Uber identified disloyal drivers by downloading information from their phones about their other activities and apps, and gave them faster and better rides, so that they would favor Uber over its competitors. In another practice, Uber may give annual bonuses to drivers that are disproportionately larger for drivers who are full time (e.g., $2,000) compared to half-time (e.g., $200). This can make drivers reluctant to work for competing companies.

Price guarantees. Best price guarantees are common to many forms of business. But the way they often work on the Internet is that they make it impossible for a company to sell its product directly for a price that is lower than that of the intermediary distributor. This means that the retail price must include the markup of the intermediary, even if the retailer is willing to sell at a lower price. The mark-up includes the commission charged by the intermediary and the cost of delivery, as with new restaurant delivery services. The guarantee that the producer will not sell to consumers at a lower price than the intermediary effectively raises prices by the amount of the mark-up. Therefore, in effect, those people who are not purchasing via the intermediary are subsidizing those who do, by paying more than they otherwise would have.

Price mechanisms work best in a market economy when costs are made apparent in them. The best-price guarantees, by hiding costs, can end up inflating prices and, if not, reducing margins of producers in favor of the margins of the intermediaries. These contracting conditions are conditions that lock the warlike profits of the Internet into the intermediaries.

An alternative would be to allow intermediaries to receive a best price guarantee that their acquisition cost for a product is no higher than when purchased directly from the producer. The intermediaries could then be required to add their commission to the basic price of the producer and to show the commission to buyers. For example, a restaurant selling a dish directly for $15 would be able to charge the platform $15. Then the platform would have to show this as the base price and explicitly show its commission, say $5, and delivery charge to the buyer. Producers would be then able to sell directly to consumers below the platform's commission-laden price and place competitive pressure for lower commissions on the platform. Those customers who search more intensively will be able to get better prices, with lower commissions, and create an environment in which customers know they should search for a good price. Such an approach could help to generate the commission competition that is otherwise missing from the market. This absence raises prices overall.

Regulating commissions and charges

When exclusives and best price rules are eliminated, it is possible that monopoly power may still remain and permit abnormally high commissions. High commissions may convert ultimately into higher prices for some or all customers. In response to durable market power, governments may wish to regulate the level of commissions and charges of intermediaries, much as governments in the past regulated rates of return on physical infrastructure investments like those in for electricity or telecommunications. If intermediaries are exploiting their monopoly power, and if their practices have broad economic effects, the argument of having a commission or rate of return regulation is strong. There should be no "internet exception" to this general rule, especially because the monopoly power effect is likely to raise overall price levels and divert funds to the platforms from companies that invest in physical assets.

For example, a regulator might find that the appropriate commission that assures a fair return on investment for an airline ticket platform is 3 percent. Then the platform would be allowed to charge a commission of 3 percent on top of its cost for a ticket, but no more.

Respect trademark owners

Intermediary platforms often take advantage of trademark owners and those who have invested to produce new assets. Such assets can include physical ones like buildings as well as intellectual ones like news. When intermediaries receive a search for such an asset, they could be prevented from diverting customer interest in a specific trademark to another company. For example, an intermediary should not be able to take a search for a rock concert of one singer, in a more prominent way, towards another concert that would attract similar customers. This is a distortion of the rights that have been created and earned by the subject of the search. Search engines could have an obligation to respect all trademarks by giving them prime position, most visible access at zero charge, including higher priority positioning that all paid advertising.

When TripAdvisor shows options for booking a hotel, it is using the hotel's investment in its name, facilities and service to attract users. The top option could be one that reflects the public service provided by search, and goes direct to the hotel, potentially *with no commission* to TripAdvisor. TripAdvisor would still be able to earn a good return on its investment while providing this public service from simple advertising or subscription services.

The reason this matters is that TripAdvisor markets itself as an information service, but is actually much more than that. Through its gatekeeper access to its system for providers, it may distort pricing up and force the restaurants and hotels to pay fees of hundreds or thousands of dollars simply for listing a link to their website. The mere provision of these links then provides TripAdvisor with a substantial share of the customer margins. The large margins are surprising to the extent that the company's investment levels are much lower than those of the hotels and restaurants. They are also surprising to the extent that most of the user value of TripAdvisor is created by external party reviews provided at no cost to TripAdvisor. Such search services could be profitable while providing a free link to direct services, and earning a share of the revenue from showing broad-ranging services that may try to redirect consumers to other sales once consumers enter their channels.

When Booking.com receives a search for a specific luxury hotel in Paris, they will then show customers other hotels in Paris. This is taking profit from the hotel that has built up a trademark and made large physical investments.

When the Apple App Store receives a search for a popular application, it generally shows another application first, in return for payments from the other application. This positioning is an example of Apple taking advantage of the investment that the popular application has made in developing and advertising its product.

The rule could be simple: any service that is providing information to the public must provide its most visible, obvious and attractive link, at no cost, to the direct seller of a product or service, in return for the right to reference trademarked services that required substantial investment. The reason for this is that trademark holders must invest to develop their trademark, but the way that search engines operate on a search of a trademarked term appropriates an important part of the gain from those investments. The search services could subsequently show other products, and other intermediaries, but these other services should not be able to make the exclusive profit from the basic investment the producer has made to create a product. If we do not give the fundamental reward for large physical investments to basic producers, the margins for individual consumers will increasingly be taken by the intermediary platforms. The basic producers, who are local, will not receive the main profits from the sale and will face declining returns on their investments, and subsequently declining *levels* of investment. At a time of great public policy concern about declining investment levels, establishing incentives that yield higher returns to investments may be needed.

Social and personal impacts

Personal impacts of addictive behavior can be serious. Often the nature of internet products creates group responses or behaviors that go beyond individual effects.

Parents are fundamentally responsible for their children's behavior. But internet companies are not giving parents adequate and detailed controls over their children's usage of these platforms. They are not doing so because their individual commercial interest is to maximize all users' time on the medium, including children. This is because they earn their revenue from having more eyeballs to sell for advertising purposes.

For example, YouTube's default program could have a feature that does not allow the default automated playing of a subsequent video. Effective time manager programs for children and adults could automatically stop access to the Internet after a user-determined time limit. Such programs could help people increase their ability to concentrate. Children could refocus on their homework, outdoor exercise and other positive activities for mental and physical development. This is not to suggest that YouTube is not useful, as its benefits to children can include much learning about the world and subjects that they would not otherwise have known. As with the link between Facebook and Instagram, some users are not aware of the links between Google and YouTube. The monetization of information from YouTube, including through advertising that reaches children, provides advertisers with a previously unthinkable opportunity to reach young minds, and affect their preferences, while their lifetime habits are being formed.

Substantial limits were placed on advertisements during children's television programs. Yet such limits have to some extent been escaped by the Internet, due in part to the difficulty of determining who is in front of a computer screen. Companies – and their boards – can be suspected of turning a blind eye to all these impacts.

The addictive behavior towards digital platforms entertainment of most children and adults helps to fuel the 200-billion-dollar powerhouse of advertising revenues maintained by Google.

Special features will help like YouTube for kids (first released in 2015) and stricter oversight of age limits on Instagram (announced in June 2022). But these features will not solve the fundamental problem of oversight, excessive time spent and declining capacities of extended concentration. Parents would benefit from the creation of one single app through which they can control, monitor and pre-establish rules relating all the videos, websites, apps and computer programs that their children are accessing. It is the traditional right of parents to control their children's education, not that of enterprises focused solely on profiting from their users.

Regulatory responses

The regulatory governance of the internet platforms and search engines should be overseen by regulators at both national and international level. The international level is important because the sales are inherently cross-border in many cases. Establishing different rules for different jurisdictions can create an extremely complicated regulatory environment.

This international regulator could be set up with government oversight of its operations in order to have legitimacy and authority. At the same time, it must be recognized that some governments will have more interest than others to restrain any undue power and abuses by internet companies.

Given the inherently incompatible government interests

in controlling the internet commerce and its gains, preventing lobbying will not be sufficient to prevent hijacking of the international government apparatus. The interest of most G20 countries to discuss internet dominance and design a response to this dominance, for example, has been made evident in past G20 meetings, such as the German Digital Ministerial in 2017. But one country stands apart. The US consistently objects to discussion of limits on digital companies. Similarly, the US has prevented, the use of the words "dominant" and "winner-take-all markets" in official international organization documents. These actions by the Department of State are a logical defense of the countries' financial interests. It is exactly these sorts of defenses that will sideline any united efforts to properly regulate the Internet.

In short, when one or two countries are dominant exporters of a good, one cannot reasonably expect that they will cooperate to reduce their own, hard-won market power. The reason is that exporters have fundamentally different economic interests from importers. Exporting countries want higher margins and higher profits, while importing countries want lower margins and better ability to tax a share of the profits. The solution that has been used by international organizations in the past to deal with a situation of such fundamental incompatibility is simple: create a limited member organization that excludes countries with dominant exporter interests. This is precisely what has been done in the creation of the International Energy Agency after the first oil crisis in the 1970s. That is, the coordination of exporters in OPEC led to the creation of a fact-gathering and policy-evaluating body that would coordinate importing countries. Norway, as a net oil exporter, has been excluded from the organization.

More generally, any new internet governance regulatory body with regulatory power would reasonably exclude net exporters of internet services, notably the US. As the top exporter of internet services, the US would inevitably have different economic incentives for all tax and economic regulation of the sectors. As a result, a structure that allowed any country to join, and pay consequent membership fees, would be of at least an N-1 structure.

To ensure that absence of a vote by the excluded countries is not replaced by client state voting, any lobbying by the exporting countries via their diplomatic or affected companies could be subject to public disclosure including the participants in communications and detailed content of all conversations. Such disclosure would be important to prevent hidden influence from becoming too strong.

Internet companies may then feel stuck in the middle. But one principle should be declared from the start: double taxation is not permitted. Profits of companies may not be taxed repeatedly. In short, if a British internet company is taxed on its profits in France, the British tax authorities should recognize that the amount paid to France would reduce the corporate income liabilities of the company in the UK.

If an international digital regulatory agency could be established, it (and potentially other pre-existing international bodies) could divide the following responsibilities:

1. Establishing base standards for national and local regulation;
2. Establishing base standards for taxation of internet companies;
3. Establishing base standards for access to data in ways that can create competition while protecting privacy;
4. Establishing base rules for ensuring privacy rights are defined and respected without adopting solutions that waste people's time;
5. Establishing base rules for oversight of search and platform activities, including for any price regulation;
6. Establishing conditions under which nations may

filter out internet companies; and

7. Obliging internet companies to provide information to consumers in case the companies are closed down.

The enforcers would need powers sufficient to apply their rules. These powers could, for example, focus on mandatory orders for companies to change their behavior, followed by fines or market exclusion for non-implementation.

Those companies affected by the enforcers' actions would need legitimate procedures for making their arguments, entering evidence, and challenging any mandatory orders or fines.

The ultimate structure and base of such an organization would need to lie outside of the US in a jurisdiction that criminalizes all efforts by foreigners to illegitimately access or influence the actions of the organization. Illegal activities would include intelligence monitoring and unreported private or government lobbying targeted at the organization, its employees or its delegates.

The creation of such an international body may be deemed unlikely. Even if it were set up, its achievements might be limited. But it might place a valuable uniform constraint on internet companies and avoid a Balkanization of regulation that now seems on course.

Ensure regulatory responses happen at appropriate speed

Up until now, regulatory responses to anti-competitive effects or privacy violations have been extremely slow. While technological development is moving at supersonic speed, regulatory response has been snail-like in its progress. If regulatory procedures and methods are now too slow for effectively influencing the rapidly evolving playing field, regulatory procedures must be changed to facilitate response that is of a speed and firmness appropriate enough to address technological change.

Examples of recent cases with slow response times have

included the main US antitrust case against Microsoft. This case lasted 6 years before yielding an outcome. The investigation was started under the oversight of the Joel Klein-led antitrust agency in 1996. The case operated under legal procedures that guaranteed plaintiff rights to defense.

The investigation into Microsoft's practices to influence the distribution of internet browsers started when market leader Netscape browser had a greater than 80 percent market share, and Internet Explorer had less than 20 percent. Microsoft was alleged to use pressure to computer manufacturers to include a default installation of the Microsoft Internet Explorer browser on new computer sales. While Netscape could be added later, it would not be in the initial configuration of software. Netscape felt that this form of "tying" was eliminating its ability to compete on its own merits. By the time the last appeal was decided on the case in 2002 Microsoft had a browser market share of about 95 percent, as shown in Figure 2. Only in 2012 did Microsoft's browser share fall below 50 percent.

Figure 2. US browser shares: 1996 – 2012

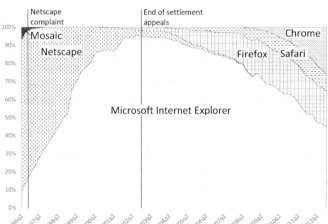

Source: author calculations based on data from ESS, WSS, TheCounter and StatOwl.

While Microsoft lost the case, and the government won, the victory for the government was Pyrrhic. The real winner was Microsoft. According to observers, it had successfully prevented the spread of an alternative interface that could have damaged its Windows operating system monopoly. This slow, six-year outcome was not the fault of the antitrust agency. It was entirely the fault of a system that is incapable of moving quickly, due to procedural protections. It is essential to protect those accused of harm; they should have the full right to present a strong defense, and we must also ensure that evidentiary standards are high for government intervention. But such protections should not permit the elimination of competition. The judicial decision making in such cases must occur more quickly. Yet the process must recognize that the outcome of a complex litigation is not known in advance. In this case, for example, Microsoft was offering a better product in price terms, with its browser offered for free not only to individuals but also to businesses, in contrast to Netscape's which was only free to individuals. This fact could have swung the case in Microsoft's favor.

The European Commission cases against Google Shopping had similarly long periods of investigation, with outcomes that effectively placed weak or ineffectual constraints on the company found to have violated the law.

But the recent record holder of a case is for the European Commission's Intel abuse of dominance case. This case began in 2002 with Intel alleged to have implemented pricing and other sales incentives that effectively reduced the ability of competitors, notably AMD, to grow at the rate that it would otherwise have grown. In other words, Intel was alleged to have acted anti-competitively to exclude competitors from free access to the market in which the most efficient provider of the computer's brain chips (known as Central Processing Units) would win market share. While the premise of the case is relatively simple, the case decision by the European Commission only occurred in 2009, and the most recent court decision, of January 2022, was appealed to the highest European court as of June 2022.

As a result, whatever regulations and regulatory procedures are put in place for the Internet, they must be designed to allow effective operation at a speed that is sufficient to address the need for true and effective regulation. Only with speedy and powerful government regulatory responses can the tidal wave of the digital war be reversed.

The possibility of more active regulation of the Internet is now becoming reality. The European Union has agreed a Digital Markets Act, the United States congress is, at the time of writing, considering major digital legislation and the UK has announced that it will, at some point in the near future, pass legislation for a Digital Markets Unit that would have regulatory responsibilities.

The differences between regulation and competition law are that regulations will, in principle, be able to move more quickly than competition law and to establish clearer standards and guidance for internet companies than currently exist. Having such standards is particularly important to make sure that companies do not feel forced to compete in a downward spiral with each other, due to the absence of rules. But a concomitant requirement of such legislation will be that companies that demonstrably do not follow the rules will be forced to comply.

The competition authorities have sought to use fines for the purpose of encouraging compliance. Such fines have shown, typically, little ability to change action. Unless internet companies start to respond to fines, the core techniques of regulators to require compliance would need to be direct oversight, not fines. Moreover, fines may create incentives for regulators to seek headlines that do not really change incentives or actions of regulated companies.

The set of regulations being considered worldwide tends

to focus only on the very largest of companies. This will occur through a formal process of designating companies as being covered by the rules. Early experience with such designation processes shows that the standards for designation are not well documented or reasoned. This view of designation decisions may simply be because the whole idea of designation is that some companies should have stricter regulation than others, a concept that is fundamentally unfair in my view. Even if the standards for designation are clear, the process seems clearly to derive from a decision that "we need to regulate the following companies" rather than the better approach of "we need to regulate the following types of problematic behavior." If there are rules, they should apply to all. Yet the initial rulebook is only going to apply to a handful of companies. These companies are exactly the main ones that have accomplished the same result as a territorial takeover. The process by which they are supposed to be tamed does not generally acknowledge this rationale. Commentators suggest the Europeans have established their criteria to capture some European companies specifically so that the legislation is not obviously targeted at US companies.

Even more short-sighted, the hope is that in foreign jurisdictions that are regulating US companies, the regulation will lead to more opportunities for home grown companies to succeed. The only country that appropriately defended its internet territory was China, which effectively placed domestic regulatory requirements on US companies and has created its own prospering innovation ecosystem and ensured balanced competition, with many examples of its own companies succeeding against foreign competition, as with Baidu vs Google, Taobao vs eBay, Meituan vs Groupon and Didi vs Uber. The Europeans had not sufficiently recognized that the advantage of the winning US companies comes from the incentive structure, financing structure and human capital in the US. The likely European approach of encouraging growth of substitute companies will, most likely, simply result in other non-European companies stepping into the void.

The US has provided funding for basic research and ensured that such research happens in competition between different universities and private consortia. This US approach was embodied in the Bayh-Dole Act of 1980. The act recognized the key role of advancement in science for the global economic competitiveness of the US. It reversed prior US policy and allowed IP generated with federal grants to be owned and licensed by universities for commercial purpose. It also allows the US government to "march in" and obtain rights to use patents if the owner has not taken "effective steps to achieve practical application" or to apply to health and safety needs. The private control of federally funded research outcomes is controversial. But the Bayh-Dole Act was followed by many universities increasing both their filing for patents and their commercialization of patents. This better university infrastructure for commercialization was used not only for federal grant-based innovation but for other university innovations. The resulting innovation ecosystem is at the core of much US technological success. In addition, the European venture capital market is disaggregated with about 35 percent of funding coming from governments and only 12.7 percent from pension funds and insurance companies. Large investment rounds to scale up venture investments are "driven by overseas investors" according to the European Commission "which results in a large percentage of recipient firms leaving the EU" or 45 percent of EU recipients between 2003 and 2015. The European proposal for an "EIC ScaleUp 100" financing would involve government selection of 100 potential future large value companies to receive government support to scale up in size and build their products. The historic problem with this approach is that government money is not smart money. A better approach would involve large scale European private financing of scaling up by European enterprises. In fact, such financing does arrive through international capital markets into private equity funds. The government funding would therefore likely target many companies that the private sector believed had no commercial future. Until Europe and other regions get their innovation ecosystems right, US technological success will likely continue. This will have the consequence that US companies are likely to fill voids left by government restrictions on existing internet companies.

We can look at the UK for an example of how European countries often move in counter-productive directions for their own innovation and education structures. In 2021 the British government forbade the use of apprenticeship funds as a source of finance for managers to obtain an MBA. This change perhaps occurred in consideration of enhancing opportunities for the less educated workers and the appropriate role of apprenticeship funds. Such changes may be motivated by the simplistic thought that increased management skills should be funded by those who benefit from them directly while other workers need more help. But the broad economic consequences are serious. While an increase in cost for management training may ensure that more company training funds go to operational and less educated staff, the effect on company management could be disastrous, particularly in a country in which management is not up to the standards of the US. Increasing the costs to individuals of augmenting their skills, without increasing their personal benefits form that training, simply leads to less such training. Increasing professionalism of business management is a clear generator of increased national economic performance. Short-sighted decisions like this exacerbate the management training gap that exists between US managers and UK managers.

Nonetheless, without creating the underlying conditions amenable to digital innovation, the Europeans are now passing regulations deemed to "tame" the internet giants.

The regulations are applying identical rules to very different situations and do little to acknowledge the differences in market power and societal problems from the companies' varied business activities that differ dramatically. Many of them are backward looking based on prior cases, and those that are forward looking are likely to end up in litigation for years. The passage of such regulation will be a necessary condition for taming the giants, but it will not be sufficient.

European Union Digital Markets Act

The core details of the European regulation are particularly important to understand, as many of them may affect internet company behavior in important ways.

The rules agreed on 25 March 2022 and passed on 5 July 2022 have the stated objective of creating "fairer competition" for digital businesses, providing consumer protection and supporting greater innovation.

The approach is based on the idea that the European Union government will have new regulations that apply *only* to "designated" gatekeeper companies. Designated companies will be established based on factors like the following:

1. Turnover above €7.5 billion per year within Europe over the last three years, or an average market capitalization of €75 billion;
2. Over 45 million monthly end users; and
3. Control of one or more platform services in at least 3 or more European Economic Area countries.

A further category of "emerging gatekeeper" is considered which can be used to apply obligations to companies whose position is proven but not yet sustainable.

An external analysis of these conditions would suggest that the lawmakers were thinking about how to ensure that specific companies would be captured by the law, and that other specific companies would not be captured by the law. Such rules clearly capture the main large internet companies. But others may not be captured, like Booking.com, or Uber, depending on the facts.

According to the Consilium information that resolved European Parliament and European Council disagreements over precise text, the designated gatekeepers will have both responsibilities and specific things they cannot do.

Non-designated companies will not have responsibilities for the so-called fair treatment that is required from the designated gatekeeper companies. That is, the rules set a two-speed law, one set of rules for the largest companies, and potentially no rules for the rest. This disparate treatment may be criticized as discriminatory, but may also be the only realistic way to start and viewed as a first step that will later be followed by broader rules.

Some of the obligations include:

1. Ensuring that users have the right to unsubscribe under similar conditions as when subscribing to services, a rule that has already been enacted in California;
2. Not installing key software (like web browsers) by default with operating systems;
3. Ensuring the instant messaging systems are interoperable;
4. Allowing app developers "fair access" to special capabilities of smartphones, like the chip;
5. Ensure that sellers have access to information on their marketing or advertising performance; and
6. Inform the European Commission of mergers and acquisitions.

Some of the activities that will be blacklisted include:

1. Self-preferencing, or ranking their own products better than those of other providers;
2. Reusing private data collected during one service for

the purpose of another service;

3. Setting conditions on businesses that they cannot sell more cheaply on other platforms;
4. Require payment over their preferred payment method, such as requiring app developers to use in-app payment systems within app stores; and
5. Bundle different items as a single package.

Most importantly, it appears that the designation process will be followed by customized regulation of each designated company. The quality of such regulation, and true principles that underlay it, remain to be seen.

The law will require interoperability of some services. Telecommunications regulation history shows that vague requirements of interoperability, such as those of the US 1996 Telecommunications Act, are followed by years of litigation.

The ultimate impact of the EU rules could be substantial but will depend on the duality of EU government enforcement practice, on the one hand, and the extent to which companies obey the spirit of the rules.

In one example related to following the letter but perhaps not the spirit of rules, in 2022, Apple was required to allow competitive payments for Appstore dating apps by The Netherlands competition authority. Apple changed some practices but was found in violation of the letter of the decision multiple times, and fined the maximum amount of five million euros each time, before Apple and the authority reached a position in which the competition authority ceased claiming Apple was infringing the decision.

The European Commission will be the sole enforcer of this legislation, meaning that it cannot be enforced piecemeal by its 27 member countries, but also meaning that non-action by the European Commission means non-action overall.

Violations of the rules could result in fines of up to 10 percent of worldwide turnover, or up to 20 percent in case of repeated violations. These fine amounts are large, and remarkably, equivalent to those applied to economic cartels.

Importantly, the regulation also has provisions to stop companies from circumventing the intent of the regulations. Such provisions, while laudable, may be too vague, practically difficult to follow and, ultimately, unenforceable.

The view of the legislators was that concerns related to data collection and market power would be addressed by the Digital Markets Act (DMA), Regulation on Contestable and Fair Markets in the Digital Sector published on 12 October 2022, while broader societal concerns are addressed under a separate Digital Services Act, the Regulation on a Single Market for digital services, which was published on 27 October 2022..

The DMA regulation is subject to enforcement 6 months after legislative passage, meaning that companies were given some time to adapt their procedures and software. Unfortunately, the narrow sector-level guidance to apply to companies would be created through subsequent enforcement and investigation, rather than prior clarity, placing companies in a situation in which they are required to follow a law without understanding exactly how it should be applied to their business. For companies that repeatedly and flagrantly violate the law, the possibility could exist of closing their access to the EU.

UK Online harms bill

In another important development to affect social impacts of the Internet, the UK Parliament has proposed an online harms bill in February 2022. This bill would create a harm-based communications offense, a false communications offense and a threatening communications offense. These are in addition to offenses related to terrorism and child sexual abuse. Further offenses would include incitement to violence, hate crime and financial crime.

Advertising services would have an obligation to prevent the showing of fraudulent adverts. These would include adverts that suggest a famous person advocates a product despite never having endorsed the product.

The rules would include a "verification duty" allowing people to prove they are adults and a "user empowerment tools duty" that would require providers to give adults tools that would allow them to control who they interact with and the legal content they can see.

The law would require the large internet access points, like Facebook or YouTube, to ensure that their content meet the requirements, and thus treat them as publishers. The exact parameters of this requirement will determine the extent to which legitimate speech is prevented and censorship becomes built into the system.

Certain of these changes impose remarkable restrictions on freedom of extreme speech which, while perhaps broadly justifiable, may have the effect of curbing individuals and groups from expressing or influencing political views that are important to them. In particular, hate speech or advocating prejudice may, from an alternative perspective, include important and legitimate political speech and expression of moral and religious convictions. While many readers may object to views and moral convictions present in some parts of their populations, it is important to remember that it may be healthier for ideas to fight between themselves than for governments to punish anyone who expresses a dissenting view on the state-endorsed morality or who provides offense to others through expression of their views. The social dangers of state and corporate censorship are likely underestimated.

These coming state-endorsed restrictions in the UK are in stark contrast to those in the US. The UK approach is difficult to understand when compared to a US Supreme Court determination that allowed neo-Nazi supporters to march through Skokie, a Jewish neighborhood of Chicago, in order to express their generally unaccepted views in a highly provocative way. Endorsing a principle of freedom of speech necessarily leads to statements being made that are not generally accepted and which are offensive. But once censorship is accepted, the bounds of its application can be manipulated by those currently in power to suppress dissent.

It is perhaps not surprising that the coming UK censorship rules would originate in the precise country where *1984* was written, a book that raised the prospect of a Ministry of Truth. England has sometimes applied its censorship rules in worrying ways. It banned the book *Spycatcher* by Peter Wright, a former UK intelligence official. The book contained controversial arguments suggesting that a former director of MI5 was a Soviet spy and that, potentially, so was a former Prime minister. These allegations were, and remain, of high public significance. But for years the government fought to ban the book's sale and the Cabinet Office still refuses to release documents related to its decision to ban the book. This example illustrates the little-perceived but serious dangers of opening the door to censorship.

US Legislation

The US Congress will potentially enact certain legislations to ensure more competition among the internet companies and to make "certain discriminatory content" unlawful. These are represented in HR.3816 and S.2992 "American Innovation and Choice Online Act." These bills would allow the US FTC or US Department of Justice to designate companies as covered by the legislation. The bill in its April 2022 version would:

1. Prevent self-preferencing, that is would not allow the covered platforms to "unfairly preference the…operators own products, services or lines of

business over those of another business user…in a manner that would materially harm competition on the covered platform;"

2. Make it illegal to condition preferential status on the purchase of another service;
3. Prevent discrimination against similar users;
4. Establish which platforms would assist and not materially impede interoperation with their platforms by others;
5. Determine that platforms would not be able to restrict access to data generated by the activities of competing business users;
6. Prevent the platform's use of nonpublic data;
7. Ensure that ranking of choices presented would be given under clear and transparent criteria; and
8. Ensure that companies or individuals could not be limited from confidentially contacting law enforcement officials.

Fines under this provisional legislation could be up to 15 percent of revenues. For companies with low margins, this could mean that they pay fines substantially more than any profits.

Where will these legislative changes lead?

The government believers responsible for passing this new legislation are confident that it will fundamentally change the balance of power between the large internet companies and citizens, thus reducing these companies' ability to control commerce. They believe the legislation will renew the promise of freedom to individual consumers.

This new legislation would be a step in the right direction, but overall we may be skeptical of its ability to resolve concerns we might have. These reforms do have the potential to alter the balance of power, but they cannot alone create the foundation needed for a healthy society. They are necessary but not sufficient.

Mistakes, unintended consequences and inaction in the face of problems are inevitable parts of government activity, as demonstrated through repeated experience. For example, the financial crisis arose from a blindness to a new form of financial instrument that was putting together toxic investments into larger toxic investments. Where were the regulators? They *were* at the wheel. The Treasury and leading banks were aware of the developing sub-prime problems as early as 2002 and considered ways to address the problem. But, on the one hand, the government wanted to avoid creation of new regulation. On the other hand, the private sector could not develop a solution on its own due to the risk the companies creating the solution would be prosecuted as a cartel for setting maximum interest rates or creating rules that clearly constrained who could borrow. The slowly unrolling financial disaster from this dual inaction only made itself palpable five years later with the Lehman failure of 2007.

We have seen government mistakes in the recent past. The privacy regulations, that have been passed worldwide over outrage concerning abuses over the considerable amount of personal information held by large internet companies, have mostly failed in their mission. They have imposed very high costs on society and worst of all, enhanced the market position of those companies that can best afford to adopt the rules. For example, some evidence suggests that in the weeks following European adoption of the GDPR, use of Google and Facebook controlled services increased by 25 percent, suggesting that the privacy rules increased the market concentration of these companies in ad technology and hurt those smaller companies that might have served as challengers. While the smaller companies eventually earned back much of their loss, once they proved their compliance with the rules, very few governments reacted when Google announced that, to ensure privacy, it would ban cookies. This blatantly anti-competitive plan, which would have made competing ad services even more difficult to operate, was only attacked by the UK competition authority, which fortunately negotiated a worldwide solution. Google itself would have maintained a superior access to information compared to its competitors, from this ban and may still succeed in doing so after the implemented part is put in place. The mere announcement of the cookies ban shows the danger of having browser technology run by an advertising distributor. But more importantly, this cookies crisis shows the unintended consequence of "protecting" privacy.

The core problem is that governments are good at responding to problems that have occurred in the past and avoiding a repeat of those problems. But they are not particularly good at foreseeing and avoiding major problems of the future. Most non-US countries are constrained by internationally agreed rules on trade and taxation that prevent them from truly addressing the economic and social impacts of the internet takeover.

In consequence, if we want an effective response to these problems, we as individuals must be part of the solution. We can be part of the solution whether we live in the US or outside the US.

Remarkably, to the extent that there is a problem, *we* created the problem.

You and me, we invited these companies into our lives. And unless we change and impose some more controls on ourselves, we will probably continue to blithely invite them further into our lives. Government action will only be effective around the edges but will not address the core of the problem.

The digital war has been won in our own homes. It has been won in our workplaces. It has been won on our own phones, computers and tablets. We opened the door.

We have bought into the internet dream. And broadly speaking, I at least think that it has been a fantastic development. But if the war has been won in our homes, that is also where the rebellion must begin.

11. POSSIBLE INDIVIDUAL RESPONSES

Weapons are an important factor in war, but not the decisive one; it is man and not materials that counts.
-Mao Tse-tung

The time has come for each of us to act.

Governments cannot do it all.

Politicians may declare that they will effectively regulate internet companies. They can certainly change the way companies operate; and it is important for them to do so in many countries. But if past remedies by the European Commission for alleged digital competition problems are reviewed, we will only find a litany of actions that achieve no fundamental change. That is, remedies imposed have not successfully re-established fair competition in the targeted markets. Consumers have stayed with Google Chrome in Europe, despite having clear choices to use other browsers. Users who are finding shopping alternatives on Google saw very similar outcomes before and after the remedy from a European Commission decision, with Google simply charging other companies for shopping positioning.

We may wonder why government action is so rarely effective.

One reason might be that the existing laws were insufficient. There might be another and simple reason: governments are not in control. Their actions can help to increase our positive freedom to choose, but it is up to us to use that freedom.

We should not expect our governments to fix a situation that originates from many individual actions. The economic takeover may or may not be viewed as a problem. That is for individuals to decide, as there are many aspects of the territorial expansion that are natural results of consumers freely responding to the options that have been presented to them.

One may argue that there are no problems at all. The benefits from the internet platforms are large, evenly spread across people and have created many new opportunities and innovations.

One may argue that there is no problem with the territorial expansion but that there is a problem if market power is obtained or maintained based on an undue suppression of competition or other uses of market power.

Others may simply argue that a US expansion of economic control is a violation of national sovereignty. But if that argument is made, we should recognize that the nature of that economic control can be difficult to describe with precision. American companies may be controlling advertising, search and application platforms, but they are not controlling the production of physical goods, nor their distribution, so it is worth emphasizing that the US expansion is far from complete and will never be complete.

Whatever the argument, my core point is simple. If you believe there is a problem, do not expect the government to solve it alone.

Internet business expansion requires customer buy in. So blaming the internet companies or the US government for the expansion would be fundamentally wrong. They have taken the economic framework and laws that existed, perhaps lobbying to modify them around the edges, and then the companies became what they are through the enthusiastic acceptance and willingness of early adopters to use their products. Admittedly, later customers may have had no effective choice.

In some instances, customers may have had no effective choice, or may have been misled to adopt a product. That is problematic.

Yet one of the suggestions of this book is that companies should not be lumped together. Even if the large internet companies are all engaged in at least one problematic behavior, it is unlikely that they are problematic behaviors of the same kind and seriousness. As a result, the solutions will not be the same. One size does not fit all.

Internet retailers like Amazon have a low share of overall retail sales, probably less than 10 percent, which must be balanced by the fact that for many products, one single large physical retailer in the US (Walmart) has 25 percent or more of retail sales. Internet retailers like Booking.com, in contrast, have a quite high share of hotel reservations, perhaps 50 percent or more for it alone. Google Play Store has close to 100 percent of Android app sales, and Apple Appstore has 100 percent of iPhone app sales.

The differences between companies' market shares are large. The nature of their products is different. The nature of their possible market power, social and individual harms are also distinct. Applying common solutions to them thus seems inappropriate.

Where there are societal implications that are unacceptable, illegitimate market power or problematic individual consequences, citizens may adapt their actions to reflect the problems they perceive.

I am a believer that most impacts of internet companies are beneficial. But where there are problems, individuals on their own will likely not affect the behavior of internet companies. Actions which are done jointly by many people have the potential to reorient the Internet against the bad outcomes and against the war-winning strategy of internet companies.

We can take actions that follow from the problems we believe exist. Possible actions related to specific diagnoses are therefore listed below. These are presented as options rather than normative suggestions of the behavior people should pursue. If you do not think there is the accompanying problem, ignore the associated actions. If you do not like the way an action would affect you, please ignore it. On the other hand, if you think that the underlying problem exists, that it is important and that you are happy with the action, it is worth considering.

The idea behind these actions is that each one should be concrete, focused and acceptable. For each diagnosis, this book lists distinct actions you can take. These are by no means the only ones you could implement. Nor would I suggest they will solve all the internet problems. But they move us in the right direction.

To control market power of internet platforms:

(1) *Use third-party platforms only when they add real value.* Affirmatively search for the best prices and quality, instead of trusting internet platforms that may have a practice of presenting information to you in a biased way that is designed to veer you towards products which give them a higher margin, rather than the ones which are the best for you. Some intermediaries have great prices and great selection; these are intermediaries worth using. However, you might choose not to use them if they are preventing direct sellers from offering you a lower price. Use intermediaries when you get something truly useful from doing so, and that is hard to duplicate through other means. When the intermediary adds little value, buy directly from the producer, particularly when

the producers make high physical investments, as with hotels, airlines and restaurants. Otherwise, these facilities pay hidden commissions to the platforms, commissions that you never see and which, by contract, they are gagged from revealing to you. Buying direct is especially important for high investment activities because these investments will no longer be profitable if digital companies take an unduly high share of revenues, leading to reduced investment in these sectors.

We need to remember that earnings keep businesses going and businesses in turn create real jobs. Given the importance of earnings, we must remember that our decisions, as customers, determine who gets the earnings. When using a platform, our customer decisions are crucial for deciding where the earning land. In practice, we have often been deciding, implicitly, to reduce the earnings of "real" producers and augment the earnings of platforms.

(2) *Contact sellers directly and relax if you lose time.* Avoid using intermediaries simply to save a few seconds or because doing so avoids a phone call. Consider calling your end seller and, while you are at it, even asking for a better price that platforms do not allow them to advertise. Saving a minute here, and another there, has its logic. But it feeds the creation of a dehumanized society; one that we don't want, one that will destroy good productive jobs, and one that distorts earnings towards third party platforms instead of providers of goods and services.

(3) *Be wary of free services and pay for real advice.* While this can sound strange, it is often better to seek professional, unbiased advice, which normally would be advice that you pay for, than free advice on the Internet. Of course, there are exceptions, as with many public-spirited blogs for example. Professional advice is worth payment. For example, free advice on investments has been found to be most often costly to investors in the long run, by veering them towards products with lower returns due to hidden commissions. Do not assume that advice from web comparison and evaluation

platforms are reliable. Not only can such sites refer to websites which remunerate them, they also regularly contain false evaluations. Some researchers suggest that as many as 50 percent of product reviews on some internet sites are fake, notably when opinions can be submitted by the public without making a purchase. To the extent that fake reviews lower a platform's reputation, the platforms themselves would like to stop these "paid-for" reviews. But they have difficulty identifying them. Many free recommendations or supposed consumer experiences are paid for by producers. In some instances, negative reviews may be paid for by a producer's competitors seeking to damage the reputation of a competing product. Similarly, it is well known that many influencers receive financial compensations for product endorsements.

(4) *Use multiple providers.* In other words, multi-home when you can. For example, don't just use the ride hailing service that you consider best in your area. Instead, try to keep the number two ride-hailing company in business by using it, even if it means waiting a little longer for your ride. This would require us to control our expectation of instant service and become more patient. Alternately, use taxis when available and safe. If we do not keep the competition alive, the pressure will go away for the number one provider to do well and give good deals.

(5) *Make complaints in the face of misleading sales practices.* Make formal complaints whenever you see false advertising or when unable to undo purchases made by accident. You should however always try to contact the company first. If a company bills you without your explicit permission, or does not send you bills, complain to your better business bureau, your consumer protection authority, your credit card company and your national political representative.

(6) *Use multiple search engines.* The reason is to help smaller search engines improve their search quality. The only way search engines improve is from having more experience of

addressing the long tail of uncommon queries. If you just use the most popular search engine, you may get better search results, but you are also not enabling other search engines to improve. This improvement, according to research by Klein and colleagues on user perceptions of quality from different search engine outputs, could come largely from the amount of usage that sites have, and only to a modest degree from having better algorithms. Ultimately, if data is truly shared between search engines as may happen under the new European Digital Markets Act which was developed to reduce internet company market power, such individual behavior to support search engine competitors might not be necessary anymore. But the ultimate success of this will depend too much on regulators.

To ensure societal consequences are acceptable:

(7) *Support local brick-and-mortar stores.* When you have the choice between a brick-and-mortar store or an online one, favor the former. Local shops may be too expensive, be inconvenient or lack choice, in which case it may be preferable to order online. However, if buying physically is a viable option, it should be prioritized. The is to help keep street stores and town shopping centers alive. Local people and families make their livings from such stores. Browsing in a real bookstore is also a fantastic experience for finding books, for example. This is not yet fully duplicated by online sellers. The disappearance of physical stores takes away, especially from children, the enjoyable experience of hunting for books, which could form lifetime positive habits of reading. As purchasing turns to the Internet, these local stores, might just disappear, like many bookstores have, and the whole nature of our metro areas could change in ways that are hard to predict. We may then move toward a world where there is no option for people to live without buying digital. At the same time as we move to buying from real

stores, we can reward "digital" companies that make street store innovations, such as Amazon Fresh stores that allow instant physical checkout without users having to scan their items. We can also favor stores that offer local natural products.

(8) *Use platforms that treat their partners well.* When using intermediaries, choose the ones that have a reputation of fair treatment towards their supply side users. Stay away from intermediaries that use high-cost transaction mechanisms, like gaming platforms with very high commissions on sales charged to the game developer. One major game platform, Steam, allegedly charges a 30 percent commission to developers. A more recent competitor, Epic, charges only 12 percent, and so should thus be preferred. Apple AppStore apps and Google Play Store often take a commission of 30 percent on sales over the store. Where you can, buy direct instead, over a seller's website.

(9) *Do your part to keep system costs down.*

-Use debit cards instead of credit cards when paying over the Internet. Debit cards have much lower fees (often 50 percent or lower) for the merchants, which helps them to keep prices down for us all.

-When buying multiple products to deliver from a single seller, select an option that allows multiple products to be delivered together. This saves on delivery costs, especially if you are not charged for them.

-Click on "natural results" from searches. These are the results that are not advertisements, and which are the search engines' predictions of good matches for you. Often, the same website will be presented as both a "natural" result and an advertisement. Do not click on a search engine advertisement for the company you want to go to if its natural result is there as well. Scroll down and find the natural result for the same company. The company pays a commission if you click on the ad, and that raises the costs for the company; these costs may trickle down to us, the consumers.

(10) *Don't post information on others without their consent.* Do not post information on other people through social media without their explicit permission. They have a right to privacy. Similarly, others should not be giving out information on you. Complain if that occurs.

(11) *Be informative when you post, not negative or insulting.* While trying to spread true information, do not try to destroy people's reputations. Do not try to embarrass them publicly. The cultural rules of politeness that apply in person should also apply over the Internet. Anonymity and distance have fostered quarrels and violence. The mere fact that the Internet gives everyone a potential public voice does not give us the right to deform other people's reputations, particularly people who are not in the public eye, nor to threaten people with opinions you do not like by revealing their address.

To limit negative impacts on individual and family welfare:

(12) *Control your own and children's addictive behaviors.* Demand and adopt simple common interface services that allow parents to control multiple device limit time on the Internet, to avoid the loss of patience and concentration skills that come from extended internet use. My sixteen-year-old son, for example, felt he was addicted to TikTok. In response he deleted it from his phone, of his own will. We can all learn lessons from such self-control.

(13) *Support newspapers, TV news and paid news sources.* Yes, that is right: tactile experience matters. News is different when you read it on paper, when you touch it, and the social value of encouraging good news is incalculable. Try it, with a newspaper that you pay for. Reconnect to the world by buying and reading real newspapers and watching mainstream television news. If you end up not liking paper news, or it is not available, subscribe to online versions of

newspapers. This helps us stay curious and aware, and funds quality journalism.

(14) *Favor face-to-face interactions.* Privilege moments of direct human connection without screens, such as at family meals or face-to-face meetings.

(15) *Place limits on your internet time and STAY HUMAN.* This can be done, for example, by limiting arrival and sending times of emails and messages to prevent being on call all the time and control connection addiction. Turn off the internet connection at certain hours by default so that you find other ways to fill your time. Bill Gates used to limit his children's usage time to 45 minutes of internet time per day. You can also turn off notifications of email arrivals at your most productive times of day and outside office hours, thus reducing known factors that create stress. You can also keep track of internet time on your phone and computer and set an objective to reduce it. Connecting with people through face-to-face interactions, and avoiding dependance on virtual interactions, are keys to staying healthily human.

If we choose to take some of these actions, they should be targeted, time specific and go away when the problem goes away. That is, positive response to these actions by companies should be rewarded, while failure to improve should be met with further actions.

Ways to implement change along the lines outlined above could follow this simple plan: First, decide what problems you think exist among the three outlined; second, take the actions that would be your individual contribution to addressing the problems you identify; third, start without delay; and fourth, continue assiduously with your new habits for at least 30-40 days, which research suggests is enough time to change habits. These four steps and fifteen suggestions can make you feel better, make others feel better and help to produce a better market environment.

12. AND THUS IT ENDS...

I once was lost, but now am found
Was blind, but now I see.
-John Newton (Amazing Grace)

The time now comes to conclude our short journey together.

I wrote this book because one of the most pressing policy question that exists today is how to address the widening reach of the Internet and the companies that dominate it. Addressing this topic requires understanding the economic forces behind this change. It has been interesting for me, in researching this, to realize how the economic objectives of warfare can be met in many ways, in modern times, without sending in an army, without firing a gun, and without blatant aggression. War, and its weapons, have constantly adapted to their time and technology. The new technology, and the fact that most economic activity is now in services, means that the control of physical territory is no longer the key to economic and subsequent political control.

I am convinced that this new internet and AI age is bringing a tremendously beneficial new world into being.

While many of the points made here may appear alarmist, they should not detract from the fundamentally positive contributions that are being made by the Internet. As more and more objects are connected, the changes in our daily lives will be profound. Will these changes go in the directions we want as a society? They can.

But we cannot duck our heads in the sand like ostriches. We cannot push back against the unstoppable tide of progress, like Luddites: the British weavers and textile workers who objected to increased mechanization of looms in the early 1800s, who did not want to accept the new machine-driven world, one that made many traditional jobs disappear and required the workers to adapt to new modes of functioning and new job opportunities. Modern Luddite-style refusals to accept the changed life from the internet may be desirable from some people's perspectives. But it is not the solution for most of us. It is not a way forward.

Above all, this book has tried to first diagnose the current situation and then propose actions that may help to address that diagnosis.

If the diagnosis is wrong, the responses are likely to be misguided.

If the diagnosis is right, it has never been more urgent to act, as the control over political forces by the large internet players extends its sugar-coated tentacles over voters and politicians.

As a quick summary, the suggested options for a way forward are:

To control market power of internet platforms:
(1) *Use third-party platforms only when they add real value.*
(2) *Contact sellers directly and relax if you lose time.*
(3) *Be wary of free services and pay for real advice.*
(4) *Use multiple providers.*
(5) *Make complaints in the face of misleading sales practices.*
(6) *Use multiple search engines.*

To ensure societal consequences are acceptable:

(7) *Support local brick-and-mortar stores.*

(8) *Use platforms that treat their partners well.*

(9) *Do your part to keep system costs down.*

(10) *Don't post information on others without their consent.*

(11) *Be informative when you post, not negative or insulting.*

To ensure individual consequences are acceptable:

(12) *Control your own and any children's addictive behaviors.*

(13) *Support newspapers, TV news and paid news sources.*

(14) *Favor face-to-face interactions.*

(15) *Place limits on internet time and STAY HUMAN.*

So far, these are just words on paper. But words can be followed by actions. It is up to you to decide if you want to act. Not only can such actions help us to feel good about ourselves; at a large scale, they can influence outcomes.

I have been told by one colleague that outcomes cannot be influenced by changes in individual behavior. I believe that this colleague is wrong. Coordinated consumer responses, if large enough, *can* make a difference. So feel free to share these 15 actions with your colleagues, friends and family. To help with such sharing, the suggested actions are in a reminder box at the end of this book. You can take a snap of that box with your camera, and then send it to your friends or post it on the Internet. I would like enough of us to take these actions so that we can influence real life outcomes. Through collective change, even at a modest scale, we can change corporate decision. Otherwise, my colleague may be right, and we will be impotent to digital outcomes.

Further ideas for beneficial actions, and other complimentary updates, will be released to those who sign up on the internet site TamingTheGiants.com.

Governments *can* do a lot to help and set the pre-conditions that enable choice. They are taking substantial actions, which is an important step. But such actions will be much stronger and more effective with individual support, and similarly less effective without such support.

One point the book makes is that, even in the failure of organized government solutions, individuals can do much to change that situation. Just as platforms can create flash mobs of people joining together in a common act, we can create common action by citizens. If citizens change the business logic of alternatives faced by these companies, we can influence them to adapt.

But such action needs to be undertaken with care. My view is that many mass movements to change company behavior are based on wrong diagnoses of problems and are unfair to the companies punished.

With knowledge and careful analysis will come the ability to act and improve this new world. We are all explorers in this new world. We all need to find our way.

I hope that together we can make the inevitably new and dramatically changed environment a better place, a more humane world, a more satisfying place to live than the one in the distant past or when we were born. I would like this to be a world where humans and their values are not displaced. I would like this to be a world where our children, and theirs forever after, will take pleasure and find meaning in life. To achieve this hope, we must all join in the battle. To win the battle, we must first know it is happening, then identify the right battlefields and the relevant weapons. Finally, we must engage. We must push for sensible and effective political reactions, while taking our own steps to bend the will of strong market forces to create more effective choice.

The internet age has been operating in a Wild West environment where everything goes. This must change, and this is in the process of changing, with governments increasingly installing new rules and overseers. The sheriff *is* coming to town.

But I do not suggest at any time in this book that

government should generally substitute its wisdom for market forces. Governments are often not capable of managing stable times well, such as the precursors to the financial crisis of 2007-2010. Why would we think they can manage times of massive change? The temptations for government to take over our affairs from internet giants risks moving us into an Orwellian world of government control over our lives. To prevent excess government, the balance of government roles is crucial. Instead of giving government broad control with few checks and balances, it may be better to harness market forces, redirect them to enhance effective choice and receive the benefits we deserve. To the extent that new government rules move toward opening closed markets, preventing individual harm, stopping societal breakup and maintaining broad freedom both of expression and choice, they are laudable. But as argued here, such rules are not enough without individual action.

Yet if individuals do not see this war, if they do not engage with finding solutions themselves, then we as a society can be sure to be the losers. On the contrary, should we engage with the challenge, we can change the course of the bounding great digital river, and then we and our posterity will only be better off.

Much more needs to be done than to protect privacy. Much more needs to be done than to avoid societal cleavage that can arise from self-reinforcing views. The fundamental changes that are needed to the empire are economic; these are the changes that government will accomplish only with the greatest difficulty.

We must be careful not to place a simple Band-Aid on a wound when instead urgent surgery is needed. We – all of us – are both the surgeon and the patient. Taking this duality into account, a delicate operation can and should begin, the sooner the better, with ourselves as the actors. While hesitation will be tantamount to failure, quick and focused action can yield a fairer, healthier internet for us all.

Taming the Giants™:
A menu of 15 individual actions to create a fairer, healthier internet

This is a manifesto for action to recover balance and fairness on the Internet.

The actions are for individuals, not government because each one of us can have an impact.

For internet platform market power:

(1) *Use third-party platforms only when they add real value.*

(2) *Contact sellers directly and relax if you lose time.*

(3) *Be wary of free services and pay for real advice.*

(4) *Use multiple providers.*

(5) *Make complaints in the face of misleading sales practices.*

(6) *Use multiple search engines.*

For society:

(7) *Support local brick-and-mortar stores.*

(8) *Use platforms that treat their partners well.*

(9) *Do your part to keep system costs down.*

(10) *Don't post information on others without their consent.*

(11) *Be informative when you post, not negative or insulting.*

For you and your family:

(12) *Control your own and any children's addictive behaviors.*

(13) *Support newspapers, TV news and paid news sources.*

(14) *Favor face-to-face interactions.*

(15) *Place limits on internet time and STAY HUMAN.*

SOURCES

This book is unabashedly not an academic treatise. Instead, it is written for the curious and self-educated reader, a reader who is not focused on abstract economic, legal or political theory. I view it as a call to awareness and, for those with the will and interest, action. To enhance readability and accessibility, I have chosen, as a stylistic matter, not to use footnotes. Note in particular that stock market capitalizations were collected in April 2022 and these naturally vary over time. I do invite readers to contact me should they find any errors so that they can be corrected (quickly) in future editions.

Having said this, there are a number of sources on which I relied and that informed the thinking, some of which could be interesting for readers who might want to dig deeper into the topics addressed. I list my selection of these below, organized by chapter. The selection is brutally restricted, and simply a personal view that excludes a lot of other very interesting work. The books, reports and papers are not intended to represent the complete list of sources of information used. Nor do they characterize the helpful conversations, over many years, that have provided further material for this book.

Chapter 1.

Brady, G.L. 'The internet, economic growth and governance,' Economic Affairs, 20(1), 2000.

Leiner, B., Cerf, V.G., Clark, D.D., Kahn, R., Kleinrock, L., Lynch, D.C, Postel, J., Roberts, L.G., Wolff, S. 'Brief history of the internet,' Internet Society, mimeo, 1997.

Chapter 2.

Brady, G.L. 'The internet, economic growth and governance,' Economic Affairs, 20(1), 2000.
Leiner, B., Cerf, V.G., Clark, D.D., Kahn, R., Kleinrock, L., Lynch, D.C, Postel, J., Roberts, L.G., Wolff, S. 'Brief history of the internet,' Internet Society, mimeo, 1997.

Chapter 3.

Bundeskartellamt, Facebook Decision, 2019.
CMA, *Online Platforms and Digital Advertising Market Study*, 2019.
Crémer, J. Y-A. de Montjoye and H. Schweitzer, *Competition policy for the digital era*, Report to the European Commission, 2019.
Ennis, S., Ivaldi, M., and Lagos, V., 'Price Parity Clauses for Hotel Room Booking: Empirical Evidence from Regulatory Change', Journal of Law and Economics, forthcoming, 2023.
European Commission Android Decision. 2019.
Furman, J., D. Coyle, A. Fletcher, D. McAuley and P. Marsden, Unlocking Digital Competition, 2019.
Scott Morton, F., Bouvier, P., Ezrachi, A., Jullien, A., Katz, R., Kimmelman, G., Melamed, D. and J. Morgenstern, Report of the Committee for the Study of Digital Platforms, Market Structure and Antitrust Subcommittee, Stigler Center for the Study of the Economy and the State, 2019.
US v Facebook. Revised Complaint, 2021.
US v Google, Complaint, 2020.

Chapter 4.

Alesina A., Reich B., Riboni A. 'Nation-building, nationalism, and wars', Journal of Economic Growth, vol. 25(4), pp. 381–430, 2020.

Beard, M. *SPQR: a history of ancient Rome*, Profile Books, London, 2015.

Centeno M., Enriquez E. *War and Society*, Cambridge: Polity Press, 2016

Gennaioli N., Voth H.J. 'State capacity and military conflict', Review of Economic Studies, vol. 82(4), pp. 1409–48, 2015.

Huankuan, *Discourses on Salt and Iron*. 81 BC.

Kennedy, Paul *The rise and fall of the great powers*, William Collins, London, 1988.

König M., Rohner D., Thoenig M., Zilibotti F. 'Networks in conflict: Theory and evidence from the great war of Africa', *Econometrica*, vol. 85(4), pp. 1093–132, 2017.

Morris I. *War! What Is It Good For?: Conflict and the Progress of Civilization from Primates to Robots*, New York: Picador, Farrar, Straus and Giroux, 2014.

Morris, I. *Why the west rules—for now*, Profile Books, London, 2010.

Tooze, A. *The wages of destruction: the making and breaking of the Nazi economy*, Allen Lane, London, 2006.

Chapter 5.

Immerwahr, D. *How to Hide an Empire: A History of the Greater United States*. Farrar, Strauss and Giroux, '019.

O'Sullivan J.L. 'Annexation'. *United States Magazine and Democratic Review*. 17 (1): 5–11, (July–August, 1845.

Schweikart, L., Allen, M. *A Patriot's History of the United States: From C'lumbus's Great Discovery to the War on Terror.* Sentinel, 2004.

Zinn, H., *A people's History of the United States*. Harper Perennial. 1980.

Chapter 6.

Acemoglou, D. and Robinson, J.A. *Why nations fail: the origins of power, prosperity and poverty*. Crown Business, New York, NY, 2012.

Beard, M. *SPQR: a history of ancient Rome*, Profile Books, London, 2015.

Chua, A. *Day of Empire: How hyperpowers rise to global dominance – and why they fall*. Anchor Books. 2007.

Davies, N. *Vanished kingdoms*. Penquin, London, 2011.

Gerring J., Ziblatt D., Van Gorp J., Arévalo J. 'An institutional theory of direct and indirect rule', *World Politics*, vol. 63(3), pp. 377–433, 2011.

Kennedy, P. *The rise and fall of the great powers*, William Collins, London, 1988.

Levi M. *Of Rule and Revenue*, Berkeley: University of California Press, 1988.

Morris, I. *Why the west rules—for now*, Profile Books, London, 2010.

Tooze, A. *The wages of destruction: the making and breaking of the Nazi economy*, Allen Lane, London, 2006.

Chapter 7.

Allen, R.C., 'Economic structure and agricultural productivity in Europe, 1300-1800,' *European Review of Economic History*, 4, 1-26, 2000.

Herrendorf, B., Rogers, R. and Valentinyi, A. 'Growth and Structural Transformation' *Handbook of Economic Growth*, 2014.

Brady, Gordon L. 'The internet, economic growth and governance,' Economic Affairs, 20(1), 2000.

Broadberry, S. N., Campbell, B. M. S., & van Leeuwen, B., 'When Did Britain Industrialise? The Sectoral Distribution of the Labour Force and Labour Productivity in

Britain, 1381-1851,' *Explorations in Economic History*, 50(1), 16–27, 2013.

CMA, 'Compendium of approaches to improving competition in digital markets' Independent report for UK's G7 Presidency, 2021.

CMA, *Online Platforms and Digital Advertising Market Study*, 2020.

Fairtax 'The Silicon Six and their $100 billion tax gap,' 2019.

G20 'G20 Digital economy ministerial conference,' 7 April, 2017.

Hufbauer, G.C. and Lu, Z. (Lucy) 'The European Union's Proposed Digital Services Tax: A de factor tariff.' Policy Brief 18-15, Petersen Institute for International Economics, 2018.

Hufbauer, G.C. and Hogan, M. 'Digital Agreements: what's covered, what's possible' Policy Brief 21-22, Petersen Institute of International Economics, 2021.

Lebergott, S. 'Labor Force and Employment, 1800–1960,' p. 177 – 204) in Dorothy S. Brady, ed. Output, Employment, and Productivity in the United States after 1800, NBER, Boston, 1966.

Piketty, Thomas, *Capital in the 21st Century*. Harvard University Press, Cambridge: MA, 2014

Rasler K., Thompson W. 'War making and state making: Governmental expenditures, tax revenues, and global wars,' *American Political Science Review*, vol. 79(2), pp. 491–507, 2005.

WTO 'E-commerce negotiations resume with call for intensified efforts in 2022,' 28 January, 2022.

Chapter 8.

CMA, Mobile Ecosystems Market Study, 2022.

Furman, J., Coyle, D., Fletcher, A., McAuley, D. and Marsden, P., Unlocking Digital Competition, 2019.

Scott Morton, F., Bouvier, P., Ezrachi, A., Jullien, A.,

Katz, R., Kimmelman, G., Melamed, D. and J. Morgenstern, *Final Report*, Committee for the Study of Digital Platforms, Market Structure and Antitrust Subcommittee, Stigler Center for the Study of the Economy and the State, 2019.

Chapter 9.

Beard, M. *SPQR: a history of ancient Rome*, Profile Books, London, 2015.
Breeze, D. *Handbook to the Roman Wall.* 14th edition. Society of Antiquaries of Newcastle, 2006.
English Heritage *Hadrian's Wall*, 2004.
Everitt, A. *Hadrian and the Triumph of Rome*, Head of Zeus, 2013.

Chapter 10.

ACCC, Digital Platforms Enquiry: Final Report, 2019.
AGCM, AGCOM, AGPDP, Big Data Joint Survey, 2019.
Agrawal, Ajay, Gans, Joshua, and Goldfarb, Avi *Prediction machines: the simple economics of artificial intelligence.* Harvard Business Review Press. Boston: MA, 2018.
Autoridade da Concurrencia, Digital Ecosystems, Big Data and Algorithms, 2019.
Benelux, Joint memorandum of the Belgian, Dutch and Luxembourg competition authorities on challenges faced by competition authorities in a digital world, 2019.
BRICS, BRICS in the digital economy: Competition policy in practice, 2019.
CMA, Facebook Giphy merger, 2021.
Crémer, J., de Montjoye Y-A. and Schweitzer H., *Competition policy for the digital era*, Report to the European Commission, 2019.
Ennis, S. 'US v Microsoft: Where did the time go?' CCP Working Paper 21-03, 2021.
Ezrachi, A. and Stucke, M. Virtual, *Competition: The Promise*

and Perils of the Algorithm-Driven Economy. Harvard University Press: Cambridge, MA. 2016.

European Commission Google Shopping decision.

Fletcher, A. 'Digital competition policy: Are ecosystems different?' OECD, 2020.

Galloway, S., *The four: the hidden DNA of Amazon, Apple, Facebook and Google.* Bantam Press, London, 2017.

Japanese FTC, Report regarding trade practices on digital platforms, 2019.

Levy, S. *Facebook: the inside story.* Blue Rider Press, New York, 2020.

Longuet, G. et al., Report at the French Senate on digital sovereignty, 2019.

Kühn, K.-U. 'Screening for Potential Killer Acquisitions across Industries,' CCP Perspectives on Competition and Regulation Working Paper 21-3, 2021.

Netherlands Ministry of Economic Affairs and Climate Policy, Future-proofing of competition policy in regard to online platforms, 2019.

Posner, E., and Weyl E.G.. *Radical markets: uprooting capitalism and democracy for a just society*, Princeton University Press, Princeton, 2018.

Schallbruch, M., H. Schweitzer and A. Wambach, A new competition framework for the digital economy: Report by the Commission 'Competition Law 4.0', 2019.

Stone, B. *The everything store.* Penguin, London, 2013.

UNCTAD, Competition issues in the digital economy, 2019.

US DOJ, Consent decree for Google ITA merger, 2011.

Chapter 11.

Orwell, G. *1984.* Penguin, London, 1949.

Klein, T., Kurmangaliyeva, M., Prüfer, J. and Prüfer, P. 'Search engines, user information and quality.' Working paper, 2022.

INDEX

Taylor, Zachary, 64
TCP, 11
Telecommunications Act,
    171
Tencent, 32, 33
Texas, 63, 64
Thiel, Peter, 81
TikTok, 75, 112, 187
Treaty of Frankfurt, 53
Treaty of Guadalupe
    Hidalgo, 64
TripAdvisor, 25, 37, 38, 96,
    126, 156
Triple Alliance, 55
Triple Entente, 55, 56
Tunisia, 138
Turkey, 70, 86

U

Uber, 29, 98, 153, 167, 170
UCLA, 11
UK, 27, 31, 37, 56, 58, 91,
    93, 95, 102, 103, 106,
    118, 119, 121, 123, 149,
    150, 161, 165, 168, 173,
    174, 177, 199
Ukraine, 86
University of Illinois, 16
University of Utah, 11
UPS, 128
US Department of
    Commerce, 19, 118, 119
US Department of Justice, i,
    175, 212

US Federal Trade
    Commission, 114
US Trade Representative, 6
USMCA, 5
USS Maine, 68
USSR, 66, 69, 70, 139, 174
Utah, 11, 63

V

Vancouver, 65
Venezuela, 68, 71, 72
Veracruz, 64
Versailles Treaty, 56
Videotex, 15
Viditel, 15
Virginia, 50, 61
von Clausewitz, Carl, 143

W

Walmart, 181
Washington, 13, 21, 65, 140,
    212
Waze, 149
Wei, 46, 47
Weimar, 57
West India Company, 50
WhatsApp, 33, 114, 149
White House, 7, 71, 140
Whole Foods Market, 132
Wilhelm I, 53
Woodland Hills, 132
World War I, 51, 54, 56, 57,
    58, 59, 63, 65, 66, 78, 96,
    137, 139, 140

ABOUT THE AUTHOR

Sean F. Ennis studied at King's College, Cambridge and then earned a PhD at the University of California at Berkeley. He has performed economic market analyses for governments, academia and the private sector, including paid work related to internet companies. After more than two decades working on economic and regulatory topics at the OECD, the European Commission and the US Department of Justice, he is now a Professor at the University of East Anglia in England. He has advised or taught in more than 25 countries and lived in London, Mauritius, Paris, and Washington, D.C. His interests include good food, European history and minimalist travel. He is married and has four children and a goldfish.

Printed in Great Britain
by Amazon

19504310R00132